The Princes

Madame de La Fayette

Alpha Editions

This edition published in 2024

ISBN 9789362091048

Design and Setting By
Alpha Editions
www.alphaedis.com
Email - info@alphaedis.com

Contents

THE PRINCESS OF CLEVES

Grandeur and gallantry never appeared with more lustre in France, than in the last years of Henry the Second's reign. This Prince was amorous and handsome, and though his passion for Diana of Poitiers Duchess of Valentinois, was of above twenty years standing, it was not the less violent, nor did he give less distinguishing proofs of it.

As he was happily turned to excel in bodily exercises, he took a particular delight in them, such as hunting, tennis, running at the ring, and the like diversions. Madam de Valentinois gave spirit to all entertainments of this sort, and appeared at them with grace and beauty equal to that of her grand-daughter, Madam de la Marke, who was then unmarried; the Queen's presence seemed to authorise hers.

The Queen was handsome, though not young; she loved grandeur, magnificence and pleasure; she was married to the King while he was Duke of Orleans, during the life of his elder brother the Dauphin, a prince whose great qualities promised in him a worthy successor of his father Francis the First.

The Queen's ambitious temper made her taste the sweets of reigning, and she seemed to bear with perfect ease the King's passion for the Duchess of Valentinois, nor did she express the least jealousy of it; but she was so skilful a dissembler, that it was hard to judge of her real sentiments, and policy obliged her to keep the duchess about her person, that she might draw the King to her at the same time. This Prince took great delight in the conversation of women, even of such as he had no passion for; for he was every day at the Queen's court, when she held her assembly, which was a concourse of all that was beautiful and excellent in either sex.

Never were finer women or more accomplished men seen in any Court, and Nature seemed to have taken pleasure in lavishing her greatest graces on the greatest persons. The Princess Elizabeth, since Queen of Spain, began now to manifest an uncommon wit, and to display those beauties, which proved afterwards so fatal to her. Mary Stuart, Queen of Scotland, who had just married the Dauphin, and was called the Queen-Dauphin, had all the perfections of mind and body; she had been educated in the Court of France, and had imbibed all the politeness of it; she was by nature so well formed to shine in everything that was polite, that notwithstanding her youth, none surpassed her in the most refined accomplishments. The Queen, her mother-in-law, and the King's sister, were also extreme lovers of music, plays and poetry; for the taste which Francis the First had for the Belles Lettres was not yet extinguished in France; and as his son was addicted to exercises, no kind of pleasure was wanting at Court. But what rendered this Court so splendid, was the presence of so many great Princes, and persons of the highest quality and merit: those I shall name, in their different characters, were the admiration and ornament of their age.

The King of Navarre drew to himself the respect of all the world both by the greatness of his birth, and by the dignity that appeared in his person; he was remarkable for his skill and courage in war. The Duke of Guise had also given proofs of extraordinary valour, and had, been so successful, that there was not a general who did not look upon him with envy; to his valour he added a most exquisite genius and understanding, grandeur of mind, and a capacity equally turned for military or civil affairs. His brother, the Cardinal of Loraine, was a man of boundless ambition, and of extraordinary wit and eloquence, and had besides acquired a vast variety of learning, which enabled him to make himself very considerable by defending the Catholic religion, which began to be attacked at that time. The Chevalier de Guise, afterwards called Grand Prior, was a prince beloved by all the world, of a comely person, full of wit and address, and distinguished through all Europe for his valour. The Prince of Conde, though little indebted to Nature in his person, had a noble soul, and the liveliness of his wit made him amiable even in the eyes of the finest women. The Duke of Nevers, distinguished by the high employments he had possessed, and by the glory he had gained in war, though in an advanced age, was yet the delight of the Court: he had three sons very accomplished; the second, called the Prince of Cleves, was worthy to support the honour of his house; he was brave and generous, and showed a prudence above his years. The Viscount de Chartres, descended of the illustrious family of Vendome, whose name the Princes of the blood have thought it no dishonour to wear, was equally distinguished for gallantry; he was genteel, of a fine mien, valiant, generous, and all these qualities he possessed in a very uncommon degree; in short, if anyone could be compared to the Duke de Nemours, it was he. The Duke de Nemours was a masterpiece of Nature; the beauty of his person, inimitable as it was, was his least perfection; what placed him above other men, was a certain agreeableness in his discourse, his actions, his looks, which was observable in none beside himself: he had in his behaviour a gaiety that was equally pleasing to men and women; in his exercises he was very expert; and in dress he had a peculiar manner, which was followed by all the world, but could never be imitated: in fine, such was the air of his whole person, that it was impossible to fix one's eye on anything else, wherever he was. There was not a lady at Court, whose vanity would not have been gratified by his address; few of those whom he addressed, could boast of having resisted him; and even those for whom he expressed no passion, could not forbear expressing one for him: his natural gaiety and disposition to gallantry was so great, that he could not refuse some part of his cares and attention to those who made it their endeavour to please him; and accordingly he had several mistresses, but it was hard to guess which of them was in possession of his heart: he made frequent visits to the Queen-Dauphin; the beauty of this princess, the sweetness of her temper, the care she took to oblige everybody, and the particular esteem she expressed for the Duke de Nemours, gave ground to believe that he had raised his views even to her. Messieurs de Guise, whose niece she was, had so far increased their authority and reputation by this match, that their ambition prompted them to aspire at an equality with the Princes of the blood, and to share in power with the Constable Montmorency. The King entrusted the Constable with the chief share in the administration of the Government, and treated the Duke of Guise and the Mareschal de St. Andre as his favourites; but whether favour or business admitted men to his presence, they could not preserve that privilege without the good-liking of the Duchess of Valentinois; for though she was no longer in possession of either of youth or beauty, she yet reigned so absolutely in his heart, that his person and state seemed entirely at her disposal.

The King had such an affection for the Constable, that he was no sooner possessed of the Government, but he recalled him from the banishment he had been sent into by Francis the First: thus was the Court divided between Messieurs de Guise, and the Constable, who was supported by the Princes of the blood, and both parties made it their care to gain the Duchess of Valentinois. The Duke d'Aumale, the Duke of Guise's brother, had married one of her daughters, and the Constable aspired to the fame alliance; he was not contented with having married his eldest son with Madam Diana, the King's daughter by a Piemontese lady, who turned nun as soon as she was brought to bed. This marriage had met with a great many obstacles from the promises which Monsieur Montmorency had made to Madam de Piennes, one of the maids of honour to the Queen; and though the King had surmounted them with extreme patience and goodness, the Constable did not think himself sufficiently established, unless he secured Madam de Valentinois in his interest, and separated her from Messieurs de Guise, whose greatness began to give her uneasiness. The Duchess had obstructed as much as she could the marriage of the Dauphin with the Queen of Scotland; the beauty and forward wit of that young Queen, and the credit which her marriage gave to Messieurs de Guise, were insupportable to her; she in particular hated the Cardinal of Loraine, who had spoken to her with severity, and even with contempt; she was sensible he took the party of the Queen, so that the Constable found her very well disposed to unite her interests with his and to enter into alliance with him, by marrying her granddaughter Madam de la Marke with Monsieur d'Anville, his second son, who succeeded him in his employment under the reign of Charles the Ninth. The Constable did not expect to find the same disinclination to marriage in his second son which he had found in his eldest, but he proved mistaken. The Duke d'Anville was desperately in love with the Dauphin-Queen, and how little hope soever he might have of succeeding in his passion, he could not prevail with himself to enter into an engagement that would divide his cares. The Mareschal de St. Andre was the only person in the Court that had not listed in either party: he was a particular favourite, and the King had a personal affection for him; he had taken a liking to him ever since he was Dauphin, and created him a Mareschal of France at an age in which others rarely obtain the least dignities. His favour with the King gave him a lustre which he supported by his merit and the agreeableness of his person, by a splendour in his table and furniture, and by the most profuse magnificence that ever was known in a private person, the King's liberality enabling him to bear such an expense. This Prince was bounteous even to prodigality to those he favoured, and though he had not all the great qualities, he had very many; particularly he took delight and had great skill in military affairs; he was also successful, and excepting the Battle of St. Quintin, his reign had been a continued series of victory; he won in person the Battle of Renti, Piemont was conquered, the English were driven out of France, and the Emperor Charles V found his good fortune decline before the walls of Mets, which he besieged in vain with all the forces of the Empire, and of Spain: but the disgrace received at St. Quintin lessened the hopes we had of extending our conquests, and as fortune seemed to divide herself between two Kings, they both found themselves insensibly disposed to peace.

The Duchess Dowager of Loraine had made some overtures about the time of the Dauphin's marriage, since which a secret negotiation had been constantly carried on; in fine, Coran in Artois was the place appointed for the treaty; the Cardinal of Loraine, the Constable Montmorency, and the Mareschal de St. Andre were plenipotentaries for the King; the Duke of Alva, and the Prince of Orange for Philip the II, and the Duke and Duchess of Loraine were mediators. The principal articles were the marriage of the Princess Elizabeth of France with Don Carlos the Infanta of Spain, and that of his majesty's sister with the Duke of Savoy.

The King, during the Treaty, continued on the frontiers, where he received the news of the death of Queen Mary of England; his Majesty dispatched forthwith the Count de Randan to Queen Elizabeth, to congratulate her on her accession to the Crown, and they received him with great distinction; for her affairs were so precarious at that time, that nothing could be more advantageous to her, than to see her title acknowledged by the King. The Count found she had a thorough knowledge of the interests of the French Court, and of the characters of those who composed it; but in particular, she had a great idea of the Duke of Nemours: she spoke to him so often, and with so much ernestness concerning him, that the Ambassador upon his return declared to the King, that there was nothing which the Duke of Nemours might not expect from that Princess, and that he made no question she might even be brought to marry him. The King communicated it to the Duke the same evening, and caused the Count de Randan to relate to him all the conversations he had had with Queen Elizabeth, and in conclusion advised him to push his fortune: the Duke of Nemours imagined at first that the King was not in earnest, but when he found to the contrary, "If, by your advice, Sir," said he, "I engage in this chimerical undertaking for your Majesty's service, I must entreat your Majesty to keep the affair secret, till the success of it shall justify me to the public; I would not be thought guilty of the intolerable vanity, to think that a Queen, who has never seen me, would marry me for love." The King promised to let nobody into the design but the Constable, secrecy being necessary, he knew, to the success of it. The Count de Randan advised the Duke to go to England under pretence of travelling; but the Duke disapproving this proposal, sent Mr. Lignerol, a sprightly young gentleman, his favourite, to sound the Queen's inclinations, and to endeavour to make some steps towards advancing that affair: in the meantime, he paid a visit to the Duke of Savoy, who was then at Brussels with the King of Spain. The death of Queen Mary brought great obstructions to the Treaty; the Congress broke up at the end of November, and the King returned to Paris.

There appeared at this time a lady at Court, who drew the eyes of the whole world; and one may imagine she was a perfect beauty, to gain admiration in a place where there were so many fine women; she was of the same family with the Viscount of Chartres, and one of the greatest heiresses of France, her father died young, and left her to the guardianship of Madam de Chartres his wife, whose wealth, virtue, and merit were uncommon. After the loss of her husband she retired from Court, and lived many years in the country; during this retreat, her chief care was bestowed in the education of her daughter; but she did not make it her business to cultivate her wit and beauty only, she took care also to inculcate virtue into her tender mind, and to make it amiable to her. The generality of mothers imagine, that it is sufficient to forbear talking of gallantries before young people, to prevent their engaging in them; but Madam de Chartres was of a different opinion, she often entertained her daughter with descriptions of love; she showed her what there was agreeable in it, that she might the more easily persuade her wherein it was dangerous; she related to her the insincerity, the faithlessness, and want of candour in men, and the domestic misfortunes that flow from engagements with them; on the other hand she made her sensible, what tranquillity attends the life of a virtuous woman, and what lustre modesty gives to a person who possesses birth and beauty; at the same time she informed her, how difficult it was to preserve this virtue, except by an extreme distrust of one's self, and by a constant attachment to the only thing which constitutes a woman's happiness, to love and to be loved by her husband.

This heiress was, at that time, one of the greatest matches in France, and though she was very young several marriages had been proposed to her mother; but Madam de Chartres being ambitious, hardly thought anything worthy of her daughter, and when she was sixteen years of age she brought her to Court. The Viscount of Chartres, who went to meet her, was with reason surprised at the beauty of the young lady; her fine hair and lovely complexion gave her a lustre that was peculiar to herself; all her features were regular, and her whole person was full of grace.

The day after her arrival, she went to choose some jewels at a famous Italian's; this man came from Florence with the Queen, and had acquired such immense riches by his trade, that his house seemed rather fit for a Prince than a merchant; while she was there, the Prince of Cleves came in, and was so touched with her beauty, that he could not dissemble his surprise, nor could Mademoiselle de Chartres forbear blushing upon observing the astonishment he was in; nevertheless, she recollected herself, without taking any further notice of him than she was obliged to do in civility to a person of his seeming rank; the Prince of Cleves viewed her with admiration, and could not comprehend who that fine lady was, whom he did not know. He found by her air, and her retinue, that she was of the first quality; by her youth he should have taken her to be a maid, but not seeing her mother, and hearing the Italian call her madam, he did not know what to think; and all the while he kept his eyes fixed upon her, he found that his behaviour embarrassed her, unlike to most young ladies, who always behold with pleasure the effect of their beauty; he found too, that he had made her impatient to be going, and in truth she went away immediately: the Prince of Cleves was not uneasy at himself on having lost the view of her, in hopes of being informed who she was; but when he found she was not known, he was under the utmost surprise; her beauty, and the modest air he had observed in her actions, affected him so, that from that moment he entertained a passion for her. In the evening he waited on his Majesty's sister.

This Princess was in great consideration by reason of her interest with the King her brother; and her authority was so great, that the King, on concluding the peace, consented to restore Piemont, in order to marry her with the Duke of Savoy. Though she had always had a disposition to marry, yet would she never accept of anything beneath a sovereign, and for this reason she refused the King of Navarre, when he was Duke of Vendome, and always had a liking for the Duke of Savoy; which inclination for him she had preserved ever since she saw him at Nice, at the interview between Francis I, and Pope Paul III. As she had a great deal of wit, and a fine taste of polite learning, men of ingenuity were always about her, and at certain times the whole Court resorted to her apartments.

The Prince of Cleves went there according to his custom; he was so touched with the wit and beauty of Mademoiselle de Chartres, that he could talk of nothing else; he related his adventure aloud, and was never tired with the praises of this lady, whom he had seen, but did not know; Madame told him, that there was nobody like her he described, and that if there were, she would be known by the whole world. Madam de Dampiere, one of the Princess's ladies of honour, and a friend of Madam de Chartres, overhearing the conversation, came up to her Highness, and whispered her in the ear, that it was certainly Mademoiselle de Chartres whom the Prince had seen. Madame, returning to her discourse with the Prince, told him, if he would give her his company again the next morning, he should see the beauty he was so much touched with. Accordingly Mademoiselle de Chartres came the next day to Court, and was received by both Queens in the most obliging manner that can be imagined, and with such admiration by everybody else, that nothing was to be heard at Court but her praises, which she received with so agreeable a modesty, that she seemed not to have heard them, or at least not to be moved with them. She afterwards went to wait upon Madame; that Princess, after having commended her beauty, informed her of the surprise she had given the Prince of Cleves; the Prince came in immediately after; "Come hither," said she to him, "see, if I have not kept my word with you, and if at the same time that I show you Mademoiselle de Chartres, I don't show you the lady you are in search of. You ought to thank me, at least, for having acquainted her how much you are her admirer."

The Prince of Cleves was overjoyed to find that the lady he admired was of quality equal to her beauty; he addressed her, and entreated her to remember that he was her first lover, and had conceived the highest honour and respect for her, before he knew her.

The Chevalier de Guise, and the Prince, who were two bosom friends, took their leave of Madame together. They were no sooner gone but they began to launch out into the praises of Mademoiselle de Chartres, without bounds; they were sensible at length that they had run into excess in her commendation, and so both gave over for that time; but they were obliged the next day to renew the subject, for this new-risen beauty long continued to supply discourse to the whole Court; the Queen herself was lavish in her praise, and showed her particular marks of favour; the Queen-Dauphin made her one of her favourites, and begged her mother to bring her often to her Court; the Princesses, the King's daughters, made her a party in all their diversions; in short, she had the love and admiration of the whole Court, except that of the Duchess of Valentinois: not that this young beauty gave her umbrage; long experience convinced her she had nothing to fear on the part of the King, and she had to great a hatred for the Viscount of Chartres, whom she had endeavoured to bring into her interest by marrying him with one of her daughters, and who had joined himself to the Queen's party, that she could not have the least favourable thought of a person who bore his name, and was a great object of his friendship.

The Prince of Cleves became passionately in love with Mademoiselle de Chartres, and ardently wished to marry her, but he was afraid the haughtiness of her mother would not stoop to match her with one who was not the head of his family: nevertheless his birth was illustrious, and his elder brother, the Count d'En, had just married a lady so nearly related to the Royal family, that this apprehension was rather the effect of his love, than grounded on any substantial reason. He had a great number of rivals; the most formidable among them, for his birth, his merit, and the lustre which Royal favour cast upon his house, was the Chevalier de Guise; this gentleman fell in love with Mademoiselle de Chartres the first day he saw her, and he discovered the Prince of Cleves's passion as the Prince of Cleves discovered his. Though they were intimate friends, their having the same pretentions gradually created a coolness between them, and their friendship grew into an indifference, without their being able to come to an explanation on the matter. The Prince of Cleves's good fortune in having seen Mademoiselle de Chartres first seemed to be a happy presage, and gave him some advantage over his rivals, but he foresaw great obstructions on the part of the Duke of Nevers his father: the Duke was strictly attached to the Duchess of Valentinois, and the Viscount de Chartres was her enemy, which was a sufficient reason to hinder the Duke from consenting to the marriage of his son, with a niece of the Viscount's.

Madam de Chartres, who had taken so much care to inspire virtue into her daughter, did not fail to continue the same care in a place where it was so necessary, and where there were so many dangerous examples. Ambition and gallantry were the soul of the Court, and employed both sexes equally; there were so many different interests and so many cabals, and the ladies had so great a share in them, that love was always mixed with business, and business with love: nobody was easy, or indifferent; their business was to raise themselves, to be agreeable, to serve or disserve; and intrigue and pleasure took up their whole time. The care of the ladies was to recommend themselves either to the Queen, the Dauphin-Queen, or the Queen of Navarre, or to Madame, or the Duchess of Valentinois. Inclination, reasons of decorum, resemblance of temper made their applications different; those who found the bloom worn off, and who professed an austerity of virtue, were attached to the Queen; the younger sort, who loved pleasure and gallantry, made their Court to the Queen-Dauphin; the Queen of Navarre too had her favourites, she was young, and had great power with the King her husband, who was in the interest of the Constable, and by that means increased his authority; Madame was still very beautiful, and drew many ladies into her party. And as for the Duchess of Valentinois, she could command as many as she would condescend to smile upon; but very few women were agreeable to her, and excepting some with whom she lived in confidence and familiarity, and whose humour was agreeable to her own, she admitted none but on days when she gratified her vanity in having a Court in the same manner the Queen had.

All these different cabals were full of emulation and envy towards one another; the ladies, who composed them, had their jealousies also among themselves, either as to favour or lovers: the interests of ambition were often blended with concerns of less importance, but which did not affect less sensibly; so that in this Court there was a sort of tumult without disorder, which made it very agreeable, but at the same time very dangerous for a young lady. Madam de Chartres perceived the danger, and was careful to guard her daughter from it; she entreated her, not as a mother, but as her friend, to impart to her all the gallantry she should meet withal, promising her in return to assist her in forming her conduct right, as to things in which young people are oftentimes embarrassed.

The Chevalier de Guise was so open and unguarded with respect to his passion for Mademoiselle de Chartres, that nobody was ignorant of it: nevertheless he saw nothing but impossibilities in what he desired; he was sensible that he was not a proper match for Mademoiselle de Chartres, by reason of the narrowness of his fortune, which was not sufficient to support his dignity; and he was sensible besides, that his brothers would not approve of his marrying, the marriages of younger brothers being looked upon as what tends to the lessening great families; the Cardinal of Loraine soon convinced him, that he was not mistaken; he condemned his attachment to Mademoiselle de Chartres with warmth, but did not inform him of his true reasons for so doing; the Cardinal, it seems, had a hatred to the Viscount, which was not known at that time, but afterwards discovered itself; he would rather have consented to any other alliance for his brother than to that of the Viscount; and he declared his aversion to it in so public a manner, that Madam de Chartres was sensibly disgusted at it. She took a world of pains to show that the Cardinal of Loraine had nothing to fear, and that she herself had no thoughts of this marriage; the Viscount observed the same conduct, and resented that of the Cardinal more than Madam de Chartres did, being better apprised of the cause of it.

The Prince of Cleves had not given less public proofs of his love, than the Chevalier de Guise had done, which made the Duke of Nevers very uneasy; however he thought that he needed only to speak to his son, to make him change his conduct; but he was very much surprised to find him in a settled design of marrying Mademoiselle de Chartres, and flew out into such excesses of passion on that subject, that the occasion of it was soon known to the whole Court, and among others to Madam de Chartres: she never imagined that the Duke of Nevers would not think her daughter a very advantageous match for his son, nor was she a little astonished to find that the houses both of Cleves and Guise avoided her alliance, instead of courting it. Her resentment on this account put her upon finding out a match for her daughter, which would raise her above those that imagined themselves above her; after having looked about, she fixed upon the Prince Dauphin, son of the Duke de Montpensier, one of the most considerable persons then at Court. As Madam de Chartres abounded in wit, and was assisted by the Viscount, who was in great consideration, and as her daughter herself was a very considerable match, she managed the matter with so much dexterity and success, that Monsieur de Montpensier appeared to desire the marriage, and there was no appearance of any difficulties in it.

The Viscount, knowing the power the Dauphin-Queen had over Monsieur d'Anville, thought it not amiss to employ the interest of that Princess to engage him to serve Mademoiselle de Chartres, both with the King and the Prince de Montpensier, whose intimate friend he was: he spoke to the Dauphin-Queen about it, and she entered with joy into an affair which concerned the promotion of a lady for whom she had a great affection; she expressed as much to the Viscount, and assured him, that though she knew she should do what was disagreeable to the Cardinal of Loraine her uncle, she would pass over that consideration with pleasure, because she had reasons of complaint against him, since he every day more and more espoused the interest of the Queen against hers.

Persons of gallantry are always glad of an opportunity of speaking to those who love them. No sooner was the Viscount gone, but the Queen-Dauphin sent Chatelart to Monsieur d'Anville, to desire him from her to be at Court that evening. Chatelart was his favourite, and acquainted with his passion for this Princess, and therefore received her commands with great pleasure and respect. He was a gentleman of a good family in Dauphiny; but his wit and merit distinguished him more than his birth: he was well received at Court. He was graceful in his person, perfect at all sorts of exercises; he sung agreeably, he wrote verses, and was of so amorous and gallant a temper, as endeared him to Monsieur d'Anville in such a degree, that he made him the confidant of his amours between the Queen-Dauphin and him; this confidence gave him access to that Princess, and it was owing to the frequent opportunities he had of seeing her, that he commenced that unhappy passion which deprived him of his reason, and at last cost him his life.

Monsieur d'Anville did not fail to be at Court in the evening; he thought himself very happy, that the Queen-Dauphin had made choice of him to manage an affair she had at heart, and he promised to obey her commands with the greatest exactness. But the Duchess of Valentinois being warned of the design in view, had traversed it with so much care, and prepossessed the King so much against it, that when Monsieur d'Anville came to speak to his Majesty about it, he plainly showed he did not approve of it, and commanded him to signify as much to the Prince de Montpensier. One may easily judge what the sentiments of Madam de Chartres were, upon the breaking off of an affair which she had set her mind so much upon, and the ill success of which gave such an advantage to her enemies, and was so great a prejudice to her daughter.

The Queen-Dauphin declared to Mademoiselle de Chartres, in a very friendly manner, the uneasiness she was in for not having been able to serve her: "You see, Madam," said she to her, "that my interest is small; I am upon so ill terms with the Queen and the Duchess of Valentinois, that it is no wonder if they or their dependents still succeed in disappointing my desires; nevertheless, I have constantly used my endeavours to please them. Indeed, they hate me not for my own sake, but for my mother's; she formerly gave them some jealousy and uneasiness; the King was in love with her before he was in love with the Duchess; and in the first years of his marriage, when he had no issue, he appeared almost resolved to be divorced from the Queen, in order to make room for my mother, though at the same time he had some affection for the Duchess. Madam de Valentinois being jealous of a lady whom he had formerly loved, and whose wit and beauty were capable of lessening her interest, joined herself to the Constable, who was no more desirous than herself that the King should marry a sister of the Duke of Guise; they possessed the deceased King with their sentiments; and though he mortally hated the Duchess of Valentinois, and loved the Queen, he joined his endeavours with theirs to prevent the divorce; but in order to take from the King all thoughts of marrying the Queen my mother, they struck up a marriage between her and the King of Scotland, who had had for his first wife the King's sister, and they did this because it was the easiest to be brought to a conclusion, though they failed in their engagements to the King of England, who was very desirous of marrying her; and that failure wanted but little of occasioning a rupture between the two Crowns: for Henry the Eighth was inconsolable, when he found himself disappointed in his expectations of marrying my mother; and whatever other Princess of France was proposed to him, he always said, nothing could make him amends for her he had been deprived of. It is certainly true, that my mother was a perfect beauty; and what is very remarkable, is, that being the widow of the Duke of Longueville, three Kings should court her in marriage. Her ill fortune gave her to the least of them, and placed her in a kingdom where she meets with nothing but trouble. They say I resemble her, but I fear I shall resemble her only in her unhappy destiny; and whatever fortune may seem to promise me at present, I can never think I shall enjoy it."

Mademoiselle de Chartres answered the Queen, that these melancholy presages were so ill-grounded, that they would not disturb her long, and that she ought not to doubt but her good fortune would accomplish whatever it promised.

No one now entertained any further thoughts of Mademoiselle de Chartres, either fearing to incur the King's displeasure, or despairing to succeed with a lady, who aspired to an alliance with a Prince of the blood. The Prince of Cleves alone was not disheartened at either of these considerations; the death of the Duke of Nevers his father, which happened at that time, set him at entire liberty to follow his inclination, and no sooner was the time of mourning expired, but he wholly applied himself to the gaining of Mademoiselle de Chartres. It was lucky for him that he addressed her at a time when what had happened had discouraged the approaches of others. What allayed his joy was his fear of not being the most agreeable to her, and he would have preferred the happiness of pleasing to the certainty of marrying her without being beloved.

The Chevalier de Guise had given him some jealousy, but as it was rather grounded on the merit of that Prince than on any action of Mademoiselle de Chartres, he made it his whole endeavour to discover, if he was so happy as to have his addresses admitted and approved: he had no opportunity of seeing her but at Court or public assemblies, so that it was very difficult for him to get a private conversation with her; at last he found means to do it, and informed her of his intention and of his love, with all the respect imaginable. He urged her to acquaint him what the sentiments were which she had for him, assuring her, that those which he had for her were of such a nature as would render him eternally miserable, if she resigned herself wholly up to the will of her mother.

As Mademoiselle de Chartres had a noble and generous heart, she was sincerely touched with gratitude for the Prince of Cleves's behaviour; this gratitude gave a certain sweetness to her words and answers, sufficient to furnish hopes to a man so desperately enamoured as the Prince was, so that he flattered himself in some measure that he should succeed in what he so much wished for.

She gave her mother an account of this conversation; and Madam de Chartres told her, that the Prince of Cleves had so many good qualities, and discovered a discretion so much above his years, that if her inclination led her to marry him, she would consent to it with pleasure. Mademoiselle de Chartres made answer, that she observed in him the same good qualities; that she should have less reluctance in marrying him than any other man, but that she had no particular affection to his person.

The next day the Prince caused his thoughts to be communicated to Madam de Chartres, who gave her consent to what was proposed to her; nor had she the least distrust but that in the Prince of Cleves she provided her daughter a husband capable of securing her affections. The articles were concluded; the King was acquainted with it, and the marriage made public.

The Prince of Cleves found himself happy, but yet not entirely contented: he saw with a great deal of regret, that the sentiments of Mademoiselle de Chartres did not exceed those of esteem and respect, and he could not flatter himself that she concealed more obliging thoughts of him, since the situation they were in permitted her to discover them without the least violence done to modesty. It was not long before he expostulated with her on this subject: "Is it possible," says he, "that I should not be happy in marrying you? and yet it is certain, I am not. You only show me a sort of civility which is far from giving me satisfaction; you express none of those pretty inquietudes, the concern, and impatience, which are the soul of love; you are no further affected with my passion, than you would be with one which flowed only from the advantage of your fortune, and not from the beauty of your person." "It is unjust in you to complain," replied the Princess, "I don't know what you can desire of me more; I think decency will not allow me to go further than I do." "It's true," replied he, "you show some appearances I should be satisfied with, were there anything beyond; but instead of being restrained by decency, it is that only which makes you act as you do; I am not in your heart and inclinations, and my presence neither gives you pain nor pleasure." "You can't doubt," replied she, "but it is a sensible pleasure to me to see you, and when I do see you, I blush so often, that you can't doubt, but the seeing you gives me pain also." "Your blushes, Madam," replied he, "cannot deceive me; they are signs of modesty, but do not prove the heart to be affected, and I shall conclude nothing more from hence than what I ought."

Mademoiselle de Chartres did not know what to answer; these distinctions were above her comprehension. The Prince of Cleves plainly saw she was far from having that tenderness of affection for him, which was requisite to his happiness; it was manifest she could not feel a passion which she did not understand.

The Chevalier de Guise returned from a journey a few days before the marriage. He saw so many insuperable difficulties in his design of marrying Mademoiselle de Chartres, that he gave over all hopes of succeeding in it; and yet he was extremely afflicted to see her become the wife of another: his grief however did not extinguish his passion; and his love was as great as ever. Mademoiselle de Chartres was not ignorant of it; and he made her sensible at his return, that she was the cause of that deep melancholy which appeared in his countenance. He had so much merit and so much agreeableness, that it was almost impossible to make him unhappy without pitying him, nor could she forbear pitying him; but her pity did not lead to love. She acquainted her mother with the uneasiness which the Chevalier's passion gave her.

Madam de Chartres admired the honour of her daughter, and she admired it with reason, for never was anyone more naturally sincere; but she was surprised, at the same time, at the insensibility of her heart, and the more so, when she found that the Prince of Cleves had not been able to affect her any more than others: for this reason, she took great pains to endear her husband to her, and to make her sensible how much she owed to the affection he had for her before he knew her, and to the tenderness he since expressed for her, by preferring her to all other matches, at a time when no one else durst entertain the least thoughts of her.

The marriage was solemnised at the Louvre; and in the evening the King and the two Queens, with the whole Court, supped at Madam de Chartres's house, where they were entertained with the utmost magnificence. The Chevalier de Guise durst not distinguish himself by being absent from the ceremony, but he was so little master of himself that it was easy to observe his concern.

The Prince of Cleves did not find that Mademoiselle de Chartres had changed her mind by changing her name; his quality of a husband entitled him to the largest privileges, but gave him no greater share in the affections of his wife: hence it was, that though he was her husband, he did not cease to be her lover, because he had always something to wish beyond what he possessed; and though she lived perfectly easy with him, yet he was not perfectly happy. He preserved for her a passion full of violence and inquietude, but without jealousy, which had no share in his griefs. Never was husband less inclined to it, and never was wife farther from giving the least occasion for it. She was nevertheless constantly in view of the Court; she frequented the Courts of the two Queens, and of Madame: all the people of gallantry saw her both there and at her brother-in-law the Duke of Never's, whose house was open to the whole world; but she had an air which inspired so great respect, and had in it something so distant from gallantry, that the Mareschal de St. Andre, a bold man and supported by the King's favour, became her lover without daring to let her know it any otherwise than by his cares and assiduities. A great many others were in the same condition: and Madam de Chartres had added to her daughter's discretion so exact a conduct with regard to everything of decorum, that everybody was satisfied she was not to be come at.

The Duchess of Loraine, while she was employed in negotiating the peace, had applied herself to settle the marriage of the Duke her son: a marriage was agreed upon between him and Madam Claude of France, the King's second daughter; and the month of February was appointed for the nuptials.

In the meantime the Duke of Nemours continued at Brussels, his thoughts being wholly employed on his design in England; he was continually sending or receiving couriers from thence; his hopes increased every day, and at last Lignerolly sent him word that it was time to finish by his presence what was so well begun; he received this news with all the joy a young ambitious man is capable of, who sees himself advanced to a throne merely by the force of his personal merit; his mind insensibly accustomed itself to the grandeur of a Royal State; and whereas he had at first rejected this undertaking as an impracticable thing, the difficulties of it were now worn out of his imagination, and he no longer saw anything to obstruct his way.

He sent away in haste to Paris to give the necessary orders for providing a magnificent equipage, that he might make his appearance in England with a splendour suitable to the design he was to conduct; and soon after he followed himself, to assist at the marriage of the Duke of Loraine.

He arrived the evening before the espousals, and that very evening waited on the King to give him an account of his affair, and to receive his orders and advice how to govern himself in it. Afterwards he waited on the Queens; but the Princess of Cleves was not there, so that she did not see him, nor so much as know of his arrival. She had heard everybody speak of this celebrated Prince, as of the handsomest and most agreeable man at Court; and the Queen-Dauphin had described him in such a manner, and spoke of him to her so often, that she had raised in her a curiosity and even impatience to see him.

The Princess employed the day of the wedding in dressing herself, that she might appear with the greater advantage at the ball and royal banquet that were to be at the Louvre. When she came, everyone admired both her beauty and her dress. The ball began, and while she was dancing with the Duke of Guise, a noise was heard at the door of the hall, as if way was making for some person of uncommon distinction. She had finished her dance, and as she was casting her eyes round to single out some other person, the King desired her to take him who came in last; she turned about, and viewing him as he was passing over the seats to come to the place where they danced, she immediately concluded he was the Duke of Nemours. The Duke's person was turned in so delicate a manner, that it was impossible not to express surprise at the first sight of him, particularly that evening, when the care he had taken to adorn himself added much to the fine air of his carriage. It was as impossible to behold the Princess of Cleves without equal admiration.

The Duke de Nemours was struck with such surprise at her beauty, that when they approached and paid their respects to each other, he could not forbear showing some tokens of his admiration. When they begun to dance, a soft murmur of praises ran through the whole company. The King and the two Queens, remembering that the Duke and Princess had never seen one another before, found something very particular in seeing them dance together without knowing each other; they called them, as soon as they had ended their dance, without giving them time to speak to anybody, and asked them if they had not a desire to know each other, and if they were not at some loss about it. "As for me, Madam," said the Duke to the Queen, "I am under no uncertainty in this matter; but as the Princess of Cleves has not the same reasons to lead her to guess who I am, as I have to direct me to know her, I should be glad if your Majesty would be pleased to let her know my name." "I believe," said the Queen-Dauphin, "that she knows your name as well as you know hers." "I assure you, Madam," replied the Princess a little embarrassed, "that I am not so good a guesser as you imagine." "Yes, you guess very well," answered the Queen-Dauphin; "and your unwillingness to acknowledge that you know the Duke of Nemours, without having seen him before, carries in it something very obliging to him." The Queen interrupted them, that the ball might go on; and the Duke de Nemours took out the Queen-Dauphin. This Princess was a perfect beauty, and such she appeared in the eyes of the Duke de Nemours, before he went to Flanders; but all this evening he could admire nothing but Madam de Cleves.

The Chevalier de Guise, whose idol she still was, sat at her feet, and what had passed filled him with the utmost grief; he looked upon it as ominous for him, that fortune had destined the Duke of Nemours to be in love with the Princess of Cleves. And whether there appeared in reality any concern in the Princess's face, or whether the Chevalier's jealousy only led him to suspect it, he believed that she was touched with the sight of the Duke, and could not forbear telling her, that Monsieur de Nemours was very happy to commence an acquaintance with her by an incident which had something very gallant and extraordinary in it.

Madam de Cleves returned home with her thoughts full of what had passed at the ball; and though it was very late, she went into her mother's room to give her a relation of it; in doing which she praised the Duke of Nemours with a certain air, that gave Madam de Chartres the same suspicion the Chevalier de Guise had entertained before.

The day following the ceremony of the Duke of Loraine's marriage was performed; and there the Princess of Cleves observed so inimitable a grace, and so fine a mien in the Duke of Nemours, that she was yet more surprised.

She afterwards saw him at the Court of the Queen-Dauphin; she saw him play at tennis with the King; she saw him run the ring; she heard him discourse; still she found he far excelled everybody else, and drew the attention of the company to him wherever he was; in short, the gracefulness of his person, and the agreeableness of his wit soon made a considerable impression on her heart.

The Duke de Nemours had an inclination no less violent for her; and hence flowed all that gaiety and sweetness of behaviour, which the first desires of pleasing ordinarily inspire a man with: hence he became more amiable than ever he was before; so that by often seeing one another, and by seeing in each other whatever was most accomplished at Court, it could not but be that they must mutually receive the greatest pleasure from such a commerce.

The Duchess of Valentinois made one in all parties of pleasure; and the King was still as passionately fond of her as in the beginning of his love. The Princess of Cleves being at those years, wherein people think a woman is incapable of inciting love after the age of twenty-five, beheld with the utmost astonishment the King's passion for the Duchess, who was a grandmother, and had lately married her granddaughter: she often spoke on this subject to Madam de Chartres. "Is it possible, Madam," said she, "that the King should still continue to love? How could he take a fancy to one, who was so much older than himself, who had been his father's mistress, and who, as I have heard, is still such to many others?" "'Tis certain," answered Madam de Chartres," it was neither the merit nor the fidelity of the Duchess of Valentinois, which gave birth to the King's passion, or preserved it; and this is what he can't be justified in; for if this lady had had beauty and youth suitable to her birth; and the merit of having had no other lover; if she had been exactly true and faithful to the King; if she had loved him with respect only to his person, without the interested views of greatness and fortune, and without using her power but for honourable purposes and for his Majesty's interest; in this case it must be confessed, one could have hardly forbore praising his passion for her. If I was not afraid," continued Madam de Chartres, "that you would say the same thing of me which is said of most women of my years, that they love to recount the history of their own times, I would inform you how the King's passion for this Duchess began, and of several particulars of the Court of the late King, which have a great relation to things that are acted at present." "Far from blaming you," replied the Princess of Cleves, "for repeating the histories of past times, I lament, Madam, that you have not instructed me in those of the present, nor informed me as to the different interests and parties of the Court. I am so entirely ignorant of them, that I thought a few days ago, the Constable was very well with the Queen." "You was extremely mistaken," answered Madam de Chartres, "the Queen hates the Constable, and if ever she has power, he'll be but too sensible of it; she knows, he has often told the King, that of all his children none resembled him but his natural ones." "I should never have suspected this hatred," said the Princess of Cleves, "after having seen her assiduity in writing to the Constable during his imprisonment, the joy she expressed at his return, and how she always calls him Compere, as well as the King." "If you judge from appearances in a Court," replied Madam de Chartres, "you will often be deceived; truth and appearances seldom go together.

"But to return to the Duchess of Valentinois, you know her name is Diana de Poitiers; her family is very illustrious, she is descended from the ancient Dukes of Aquitaine, her grandmother was a natural daughter of Lewis the XI, and in short she possesses everything that is great in respect of birth. St. Valier, her father, had the unhappiness to be involved in the affair of the Constable of Bourbon, which you have heard of; he was condemned to lose his head, and accordingly was conducted to the scaffold: his daughter, viz., the Duchess, who was extremely beautiful, and who had already charmed the late King, managed so well, I don't know by what means, that she obtained her father's life; the pardon was brought him at the moment he was expecting the fatal blow; but the pardon availed little, for fear had seized him so deeply, that it bereft him of his senses, and he died a few days after. His daughter appeared at Court as the King's mistress; but the Italian expedition, and the imprisonment of the present Prince, were interruptions to his love affair. When the late King returned from Spain, and Madam the Regent went to meet him at Bayonne, she brought all her maids of honour with her, among whom was Mademoiselle de Pisselen, who was since Duchess d'Etampes; the King fell in love with her, though she was inferior in birth, wit and beauty to the Duchess of Valentinois, and had no advantage above her but that of being very young. I have heard her say several times, that she was born the same day Diana de Poitiers was married, but she spoke this in the malice of her heart, and not as what she knew to be true; for I am much mistaken, if the Duchess of Valentinois did not marry Monsieur de Breze, at the same time that the King fell in love with Madam d'Etampes. Never was a greater hatred than that between these two ladies; the Duchess could not pardon Madam d'Etampes for having taken from her the title of the King's mistress; and Madam d'Etampes was violently jealous of the Duchess, because the King still kept correspondence with her. That Prince was by no means constant to his mistresses; there was always one among them that had the title and honours of mistress, but the ladies of the small band, as they were styled, shared his favour by turns. The loss of the Dauphin, his son, who died at Tournon, and was thought to be poisoned, extremely afflicted him; he had not the same affection and tenderness for his second son, the present King; he imagined he did not see in him spirit and vivacity enough, and complained of it one day to the Duchess of Valentinois, who told him she would endeavour to raise a passion in him for her, in order to make him more sprightly and agreeable. She succeeded in it, as you see, and this passion is now of above twenty years' duration, without being changed either by time or incidents.

"The late King at first opposed it; and whether he had still love enough left for the Duchess of Valentinois to be jealous, or whether he was urged on by the Duchess d'Etampes, who was in despair upon seeing the Dauphin so much attached to her enemy, it is certain he beheld this passion with an indignation and resentment, that showed itself every day by something or other. The Dauphin neither valued his anger or his hatred, nor could anything oblige him either to abate or conceal his flame, so that the King was forced to accustom himself to bear it with patience. This opposition of his to his father's will, withdrew his affections from him more and more, and transferred them to his third son, the Duke of Orleans, who was a Prince of a fine person full of fire and ambition, and of a youthful heat which wanted to be moderated; however, he would have made a very great Prince, had he arrived to a more ripened age.

"The rank of eldest, which the Dauphin held, and the King's favour which the Duke of Orleans was possessed of, created between them a sort of emulation, that grew by degrees to hatred. This emulation began from their infancy, and was still kept up in its height. When the Emperor passed through France, he gave the preference entirely to the Duke of Orleans, which the Dauphin resented so bitterly, that while the Emperor was at Chantilli, he endeavoured to prevail with the Constable to arrest him without waiting for the King's orders, but the Constable refused to do it: however, the King afterwards blamed him for not following his son's advice, and when he banished him the Court, that was one of the principal reasons for it.

"The discord between the two brothers put Madam d'Etampes upon the thought of strengthening herself with the Duke of Orleans, in order to support her power with the King against the Duchess of Valentinois; accordingly she succeeded in it, and that young Prince, though he felt no emotions of love for her, entered no less into her interest, than the Dauphin was in that of Madam de Valentinois. Hence rose two factions at Court, of such a nature as you may imagine, but the intrigues of them were not confined to the quarrels of women.

"The Emperor, who continued to have a great friendship for the Duke of Orleans, had offered several times to make over to him the Duchy of Milan. In the propositions which were since made for the peace, he gave hopes of assigning him the seventeen provinces, with his daughter in marriage. The Dauphin neither approved of the peace or the marriage, and in order to defeat both he made use of the Constable, for whom he always had an affection, to remonstrate to the King of what importance it was not to give his successor a brother so powerful as the Duke of Orleans would be with the alliance of the Emperor and those countries; the Constable came the more easily into the Dauphin's sentiments, as they were opposite to those of Madam d'Etampes, who was his declared enemy, and who vehemently wished for the promotion of the Duke of Orleans.

"The Dauphin commanded at that time the King's Army in Champaign, and had reduced that of the Emperor to such extremities, that it must have entirely perished, had not the Duchess d'Etampes, for fear too great successes should make us refuse peace, and the Emperor's alliance in favour of the Duke of Orleans, secretly advised the enemy to surprise Espemai and Cheteau-Thieni, in which places were great magazines of provisions; they succeeded in the attempt, and by that means saved their whole army.

"This Duchess did not long enjoy the success of her treason. A little after the Duke of Orleans died at Farmontiers of a kind of contagious distemper: he was in love with one of the finest women of the Court, and was beloved by her. I will not mention her name, because she has since lived with so much discretion, and has so carefully concealed the passion she had for that Prince, that one ought to be tender of her reputation. It happened she received the news of her husband's death at the same time as she heard of the Duke's, so that she had that pretext to enable her to conceal her real sorrow, without being at the trouble of putting any constraint upon herself.

"The King did not long survive the Prince his son; he died two years after; he recommended to the Dauphin to make use of the Cardinal de Tournon and the Admiral d'Annebault, but said nothing at all of the Constable, who was then in banishment at Chantilli. Nevertheless the first thing the King his son did was to recall him, and make him his Prime Minister.

"Madam d'Etampes was discarded, and received all the ill treatment she could possibly expect from an enemy so very powerful; the Duchess of Valentinois amply revenged herself both of that lady, and all those who had disobliged her; she seemed to reign more absolute in the King's heart than she did even when he was Dauphin. During the twelve years' reign of this Prince she has been absolute in everything; she disposes of all governments and offices of trust and power; she has disgraced the Cardinal de Tournon, the Chancellor, and Villeroy; those who have endeavoured to open the King's mind with respect to her conduct, have been undone in the attempt; the Count de Taix, great Master of the Ordnance, who had no kindness for her, could not forbear speaking of her gallantries, and particularly of that with the Count de Brissac, of whom the King was already very jealous. Nevertheless she contrived things so well, that the Count de Taix was disgraced, and his employment taken from him; and what is almost incredible, she procured it to be given to the Count de Brissac, and afterwards made him a Mareschal of France. Notwithstanding, the King's jealousy increased to such a height, that lie could no longer suffer him to continue at Court: this passion of jealousy, which is fierce and violent in other men, is gentle and moderate in him through the great respect he has for his mistress, and therefore he did not go about to remove his rival, but under the pretext of giving him the Government of Piemont. He has lived there several years; last winter he returned to Paris, under pretence of demanding troops and other necessaries for the Army he commands; the desire of seeing the Duchess of Valentinois again, and the fear of being forgotten by her, was perhaps the principal motive of this journey. The King received him very coldly; Messieurs de Guise, who have no kindness for him, but dare not show it on account of the Duchess, made use of Monsieur the Viscount, her declared enemy, to prevent his obtaining what he came to demand. It was no difficult matter to do him hurt. The King hated him, and was uneasy at his presence, so that he was obliged to return to Piemont without any benefit from his journey, except perhaps that of rekindling in the heart of the Duchess the flame which absence began to extinguish. The King has had a great many other subjects of jealousy, but either he has not been informed of them, or has not dared to complain of them.

"I don't know, daughter," added Madam de Chartres, "if I have not already told you more of these things, than you desired to know." "I am far, Madam, from complaining of that," replied the Princess of Cleves, "and if it was not for fear of being importunate, I should yet desire to be informed of several circumstances I am ignorant of."

The Duke de Nemours' passion for Madam de Cleves was at first so violent, that he had no relish left for any of the ladies he paid his addresses to before, and with whom he kept a correspondence during his absence; he even lost all remembrance of his engagements with them, and not only made it his business to find out excuses to break with them, but had not the patience to hear their complaints, or make any answer to the reproaches they laid upon him. The Queen-Dauphin herself, for whom his regards had been very tender, could no longer preserve a place in that heart which was now devoted to the Princess of Cleves. His impatience of making a tour to England began to abate, and he showed no earnestness in hastening his equipage. He frequently went to the Queen-Dauphin's Court, because the Princess of Cleves was often there, and he was very easy in leaving people in the opinion they had of his passion for that Queen; he put so great a value on Madam de Cleves, that he resolved to be rather wanting in giving proofs of his love, than to hazard its being publicly known; he did not so much as speak of it to the Viscount de Chartres, who was his intimate friend, and from whom he concealed nothing; the truth is, he conducted this affair with so much discretion, that nobody suspected he was in love with Madam de Cleves, except the Chevalier de Guise; and she would scarcely have perceived it herself, if the inclination she had for him had not led her into a particular attention to all his actions, but which she was convinced of it.

She no longer continued to have the same disposition to communicate to her mother what she thought concerning the Duke de Nemours, as she had to talk to her about her other lovers; though she had no settled design of concealing it from her, yet she did not speak of it. Madam de Chartres, however, plainly perceived the Duke's attachment to her daughter, as well as her daughter's inclination for him; the knowledge of this could not but sensibly afflict her, nor could she be ignorant of the danger this young lady was in, in being beloved by, and loving so accomplished a person as the Duke de Nemours: she was entirely confirmed in the suspicion she had of this business, by an incident which fell out a few days after.

The Mareschal de St. Andre, who took all opportunities to show his magnificence, desired the King, under pretence of showing him his house which was just finished, to do him the honour to sup there with the two Queens. The Mareschal was also very glad to display, in the sight of the Princess of Cleves, that splendid and expensive manner of life, which he carried to so great a profusion.

Some days before that appointed for the entertainment, the Dauphin, who had an ill state of health, found himself indisposed, and saw nobody; the Queen-Dauphin had spent all that day with him; and in the evening, upon his growing better, all the persons of quality that were in the anti-chamber were admitted; the Queen-Dauphin returned to her own apartment, where she found Madam de Cleves and some other ladies, with whom she lived in familiarity.

It being already very late, and not being dressed, she did not wait upon the Queen, but gave out that she was not to be seen, and ordered her jewels to be brought, in order to choose out some for the Mareschal de St. Andre's Ball, and present the Princess of Cleves with some, as she had promised her. While they were thus employed, the Prince of Conde entered; his great quality gave him free access everywhere. "Doubtless," said the Queen-Dauphin, "you come from the King my husband, what are they doing there?"

"Madam," said he, "they are maintaining a dispute against the Duke of Nemours, and he defends the argument he undertook with so much warmth, that he must needs be very much interested in it; I believe he has some mistress that gives him uneasiness by going to balls, so well satisfied he is that it is a vexatious thing to a lover to see the person he loves in those places."

"How," replied the Queen-Dauphin, "would not the Duke de Nemours have his mistress go to a ball? I thought that husbands might wish their wives would not go there; but as for lovers, I never imagined they were of that opinion." "The Duke de Nemours finds," answered the Prince of Conde, "that nothing is so insupportable to lovers as balls, whether they are beloved again, or whether they are not. He says, if they are beloved they have the chagrin to be loved the less on this account for several days; that there is no woman, whom her anxiety for dress does not divert from thinking on her lover; that they are entirely taken up with that one circumstance, that this care to adorn themselves is for the whole world, as well as for the man they favour; that when they are at a ball, they are desirous to please all who look at them; and that when they triumph in their beauty, they experience a joy to which their lovers very little contribute. He argues further, that if one is not beloved, it is a yet greater torment to see one's mistress at an assembly; that the more she is admired by the public, the more unhappy one is not to be beloved, and that the lover is in continual fear lest her beauty should raise a more successful passion than his own; lastly he finds, there is no torment equal to that of seeing one's mistress at a ball, unless it be to know that she is there, and not to be there one's self."

Madam de Cleves pretended not to hear what the Prince of Conde said, though she listened very attentively; she easily saw what part she had in the Duke of Nemours's opinion, and particularly as to what he said of the uneasiness of not being at a ball where his mistress was, because he was not to be at that of the Mareschal de St. Andre, the King having sent him to meet the Duke of Ferrara.

The Queen-Dauphin, and the Prince of Conde, not going into the Duke's opinion, were very merry upon the subject. "There is but one occasion, Madam," said the Prince to her, "in which the Duke will consent his mistress should go to a ball, and that is when he himself gives it. He says, that when he gave your Majesty one last year, his mistress was so kind as to come to it, though seemingly only to attend you; that it is always a favour done to a lover, to partake of an entertainment which he gives; that it is an agreeable circumstance for him to have his mistress see him preside in a place where the whole Court is, and see him acquit himself well in doing the honours of it." "The Duke de Nemours was in the right," said the Queen-Dauphin, smiling, "to approve of his mistress's being at his own ball; there was then so great a number of ladies, whom he honoured with the distinction of that name, that if they had not come, the assembly would have been very thin."

The Prince of Conde had no sooner begun to relate the Duke de Nemours's sentiments concerning assemblies, but Madam de Cleves felt in herself a strong aversion to go to that of the Mareschal de St. Andre. She easily came into the opinion, that a woman ought not to be at an entertainment given by one that professed love to her, and she was very glad to find out a reason of reservedness for doing a thing which would oblige the Duke of Nemours. However, she carried away with her the ornaments which the Queen-Dauphin had given her; but when she showed them her mother, she told her that she did not design to make use of them; that the Mareschal de St. Andre took a great deal of pains to show his attachment to her, and she did not doubt he would be glad to have it believed that a compliment was designed her in the entertainment he gave the King, and that under the pretence of doing the honours of his house, he would show her civilities which would be uneasy to her.

Madam de Chartres for some time opposed her daughter's opinion, as thinking it very singular; but when she saw she was obstinate in it, she gave way, and told her, that in that case she ought to pretend an indisposition as an excuse for not going to the ball, because the real reasons which hindered her would not be approved of; and care ought to be taken that they should not be suspected.

Madam de Cleves voluntarily consented to pass some days at her mother's, in order not to go to any place where the Duke of Nemours was not to be. However the Duke set out, without the pleasure of knowing she would not be at the ball.

The day after the ball he returned, and was informed that she was not there; but as he did not know the conversation he had at the Dauphin's Court had been repeated to her, he was far from thinking himself happy enough to have been the reason of her not going.

The day after, while he was at the Queen's apartments, and talking to the Queen-Dauphin, Madam de Chartres and Madam de Cleves came in. Madam de Cleves was dressed a little negligently, as a person who had been indisposed, but her countenance did not at all correspond with her dress. "You look so pretty," says the Queen-Dauphin to her, "that I can't believe you have been ill; I think the Prince of Conde, when he told us the Duke de Nemours's opinion of the ball, persuaded you, that to go there would be doing a favour to the Mareschal de St. Andre, and that that's the reason which hindered you from going." Madam de Cleves blushed, both because the Queen-Dauphin had conjectured right, and because she spoke her conjecture in the presence of the Duke de Nemours.

Madam de Chartres immediately perceived the true reason, why her daughter refused to go to the ball; and to prevent the Duke de Nemours discovering it, as well as herself, she took up the discourse after a manner that gave what she said an air of truth.

"I assure you, Madam," said she to the Queen-Dauphin, "that your Majesty has done my daughter more honour than she deserves; she was really indisposed, but I believe, if I had not hindered her, she would not have failed to wait on you, and to show herself under any disadvantages, for the pleasure of seeing what there was extraordinary at yesterday's entertainment." The Queen-Dauphin gave credit to what Madam de Chartres said but the Duke de Nemours was sorry to find so much probability in it nevertheless, the blushes of the Princess of Cleves made him suspect, that what the Queen-Dauphin had said was not altogether false. The Princess of Cleves at first was concerned the Duke had any room to believe it was he who had hindered her from going to the Mareschal de

St. Andre; but afterwards she was a little chagrined that her mother had entirely taken off the suspicion of it.

Though the Congress of Cercamp had been broken off, the negotiations for the peace were continued, and things were so disposed, that towards the latter end of February the conferences were reassumed at Chateau-Cambresis; the same plenipotentiaries were sent as before, and the Mareschal de St. Andre being one, his absence freed the Duke de Nemours from a rival, who was formidable rather from his curiosity in observing those who addressed to Madam de Cleves, than from any advances he was capable of making himself in her favour.

Madam de Chartres was not willing to let her daughter see that she knew her sentiments for the Duke, for fear of making herself suspected in some things which she was very desirous to tell her.

One day she set herself to talk about him, and a great deal of good she said of him, but mixed with it abundance of sham praises, as the prudence he showed in never falling in love, and how wise he was to make the affair of women and love an amusement instead of a serious business: "It is not," added she, "that he is not suspected to have a very uncommon passion for the Queen-Dauphin; I observe he visits her very often; and I advise you to avoid, as much as possible, speaking to him, and especially in private; because, since the Queen-Dauphin treats you as she does, it would be said, that you are their confidant; and you know how disagreeable that sort of reputation is: I'm of opinion, if this report continues, that you should not visit the Queen-Dauphin so often, in order to avoid involving yourself in adventures of gallantry."

The Princess of Cleves had never heard before of the amour between the Duke de Nemours and the Queen-Dauphin; she was so much surprised at what her mother had told her, and seemed to see so plainly how she had been mistaken in her thoughts about the Duke, that she changed countenance. Madam de Chartres perceived it. Visitors came in that moment; and the Princess of Cleves retired to her own apartment, and shut herself up in her closet.

One can't express the grief she felt to discover, by what her mother had been just saying, the interest her heart had in the Duke de Nemours; she had not dared as yet to acknowledge it to her secret thoughts; she then found, that the sentiments she had for him were such as the Prince of Cleves had required of her; she perceived how shameful it was to entertain them for another, and not for a husband that deserved them; she found herself under the utmost embarrassment, and was dreadfully afraid lest the Duke should make use of her only as a means to come at the Queen-

Dauphin, and it was this thought determined her to impart to her mother something she had not yet told her.

The next morning she went into her mother's chamber to put her resolves in execution, but she found Madam de Chartres had some touches of a fever, and therefore did not think proper to speak to her: this indisposition however appeared to insignificant, that Madam de Cleves made no scruple after dinner to visit the Queen-Dauphin; she was in her closet with two or three ladies of her most familiar acquaintance. "We were speaking," said she to her, as soon as she saw her, "of the Duke de Nemours, and were admiring how much he's changed since his return from Brussels; before he went there, he had an infinite number of mistresses, and it was his own fault, for he showed an equal regard to those who had merit, and to those who had none; since his return he neither knows the one nor the other; there never was so great a change; I find his humour is changed too, and that he is less gay than he used to be."

The Princess of Cleves made no answer; and it shocked her to think she should have taken all that they said of the change in the Duke for proofs of his passion for her, had she not been undeceived; she felt in herself some little resentment against the Queen-Dauphin, for endeavouring to find out reasons, and seeming surprised at a thing, which she probably knew more of than anyone else; she could not forbear showing something of it; and when the other ladies withdrew, she came up and told her in a low voice, "And is it I, Madam, you have been pointing at, and have you a mind to conceal, that you are she who has made such an alteration in the conduct of the Duke of Nemours?" "You do me injustice," answered the Queen-Dauphin, "you know I conceal nothing from you; it is true the Duke of Nemours, before he went to Brussels, had, I believe, an intention to let me know he did not hate me; but since his return, it has not so much as appeared that he remembers anything of what he has done; and I acknowledge I have a curiosity to know what it is has changed him so: it would not be very difficult for me to unravel this affair," added she; "the Viscount de Chartres, his intimate friend, is in love with a lady with whom I have some power, and I'll know by that means the occasion of this alteration." The Queen-Dauphin spoke with an air of sincerity which convinced the Princess of Cleves, and in spite of herself she found her mind in a more calm and pleasing situation than it had been in before.

When she returned to her mother, she heard she was a great deal worse than she had left her; her fever was redoubled, and the days following it increased to so great a degree, that she was thought to be in danger. Madam de Cleves was in extreme grief on this occasion, and never stirred out of her mother's chamber. The Prince of Cleves was there too almost every day and all day long, partly out of affection to Madam de

Chartres, and partly to hinder his lady from abandoning herself to sorrow, but chiefly that he might have the pleasure of seeing her, his passion not being at all diminished.

The Duke de Nemours, who had always had a great friendship for the Prince of Cleves, had not failed to show it since his return from Brussels; during the illness of Madam de Chartres he frequently found means to see the Princess of Cleves, pretending to want her husband, or to come to take him out to walk; he enquired for him at such hours as he knew very well he was not at home, and under pretence of waiting for him stayed in Madam de Cleves's anti-chamber, where there were always a great many people of quality; Madam de Cleves often came there, and her grief did not make her seem less handsome in the eyes of the Duke de Nemours; he made her sensible what interest he had in her affliction, and spoke to her with so submissive an air, that he easily convinced her, that the Queen-Dauphin was not the person he was in love with.

The seeing him at once gave her grief and pleasure; but when she no longer saw him, and reflected that the charm he carried about him when present, was an introduction to love, she was very near imagining she hated him, out of the excessive grief which that thought gave her.

Madam de Chartres still grew worse and worse, so that they began to despair of her life; she heard what the physicians told her concerning the danger she was in with a courage worthy her virtue, and her piety. After they were gone, she caused everybody to retire, and sent for Madam de Cleves.

"We must part, my dear daughter," said she, stretching out her hand to her; "the danger I leave you in, and the occasion you have for me, adds to the regret I have to leave you: you have a passion for the Duke de Nemours; I do not desire you to confess it; I am no longer in a condition to make use of that sincerity for your good; I have perceived this inclination a great while, but was not willing to speak to you of it at first, for fear of making you discover it yourself; you know it at present but too well; you are upon the brink of a precipice; great efforts must be used, and you must do great violence to your heart to save yourself: reflect what you owe to your husband; reflect what you owe to yourself, and think that you are going to lose that reputation which you have gained, and which I have so much at heart; call up, my dear daughter, all your courage and constancy; retire from Court; oblige your husband to carry you away; do not be afraid of taking such resolutions, as being too harsh and difficult; however frightful they may appear at first, they will become more pleasant in time, than the misfortunes that follow gallantry: if any other motives than those of duty and virtue could have weight with you, I should tell you that if anything were capable of disturbing the happiness I hope for in the next world, it would be to see you fall like other women; but if this calamity must necessarily happen, I shall meet death with joy, as it will hinder me from being a witness of it."

Madam de Cleves bathed with tears her mother's hand, which she held fast locked in her own; nor was Madam de Chartres less moved. "Adieu, dear daughter," said she, "let us put an end to a conversation which melts us both; and remember, if you are able, all that I have been saying to you."

When she had spoke this, she turned herself on the other side, and ordered her daughter to call her women, being unwilling either to hear her reply, or to speak any more. Madam de Cleves went out of her presence in a condition one need not describe; and Madam de Chartres thought of nothing but preparing herself for death: she lived two days longer, during which she would not see her daughter again; her daughter was the only thing she had reluctance to part with.

Madam de Cleves was in the utmost affliction; her husband did not leave her, and no sooner was her mother expired, but he carried her into the country, that she might not have in her eye a place which could serve only to sharpen her sorrow, which was scarce to be equalled. Though tenderness and gratitude had the greatest share in her griefs, yet the need which she found she had of her mother to guard her against the Duke of Nemours added no small weight to them; she found she was unhappy in being left to herself, at a time when she was so little mistress of her own affections, and when she so much wished for somebody to pity and encourage her. The Prince of Cleves's behaviour to her on this occasion, made her wish more ardently than ever, never to fail in her duty to him; she also expressed more friendship and affection for him than she had done before; she would not suffer him to leave her, and she seemed to think that his being constantly with her could defend her against the Duke of Nemours.

The Duke came to see the Prince of Cleves in the country; he did what he could to pay a visit also to Madam de Cleves, but she refused to receive him; and being persuaded she could not help finding something dangerously lovely in him, she made a strong resolution to forbear seeing him, and to avoid all occasions of it that were in her power.

The Prince of Cleves went to Paris to make his Court, and promised his lady to return the next day, but however he did not return till the day after. "I expected you yesterday," said Madam de Cleves to him on his arrival, "and I ought to chide you for not having come as you promised; you know, if I was capable of feeling a new affliction in the condition I am in, it would be the death of Madam de Tournon, and I have heard of it this morning; I should have been concerned, though I had not known her; it is a melting consideration to think that a lady so young and handsome as she, should be dead in two days; but besides, she was the person in the world that pleased me most, and who appeared to have discretion equal to her beauty."

"I am sorry I could not return yesterday," replied the Prince of Cleves, "but my presence was so necessary to the consolation of an unhappy man, that it was impossible for me to leave him. As for Madam de Tournon, I do not advise you not to be concerned for her, if you lament her as a woman full of discretion, and worthy of your esteem." "You surprise me," answered Madam de Cleves, "I have heard you say several times, that there was not a lady at Court you had a greater respect for." "It is true," replied he, "but women are incomprehensible, and when I have seen them all, I think myself so happy in having you, that I cannot enough admire my good fortune." "You esteem me more than I deserve," answered Madam de Cleves, "you have not had experience enough yet to pronounce me worthy of you; but tell me, I beseech you, what it is has undeceived you with respect to Madam de Tournon." "I have been undeceived a great while," replied he, "and I know that she was in love with the Count de Sancerre, and that she gave him room to hope she would marry him." "I can't believe," said Madam de Cleves, "that Madam de Tournon, after so extraordinary an aversion as she has shown to marriage from the time she became a widow, and after the public declarations she has made that she would never marry again, should give hopes to Sancerre." "If she had given hopes to him only," replied the Prince of Cleves, "the wonder had not been so great; but what is surprising is, that she gave hopes likewise to Etouteville at the same time: I'll let you know the whole history of this matter."

II

"You know the friendship, there is betwixt Sancerre and me. Nevertheless about two years ago he fell in love with Madam de Tournon, and concealed it from me with as much care as from the rest of the world; I had not the least suspicion of it. Madam de Tournon as yet appeared inconsolable for the death of her husband, and lived in retirement with great austerity. Sancerre's sister was in a manner the only person she saw, and it was at her lodgings he became in love with her.

"One evening there was to be play at the Louvre, and the actors only waited for the coming of the King and Madam de Valentinois, when word was brought that she was indisposed, and that the King would not come. It was easy to see that the Duchess's indisposition was nothing but some quarrel with the King; everyone knew the jealousy he had had of the Mareschal de Brisac during his continuance at Court, but he had been set out some days on his return to Piemont, and one could not imagine what was the occasion of this falling out.

"While I was speaking of this to Sancerre, Monsieur d'Anville came into the room, and told me in a whisper, that the King was so exasperated and so afflicted at the same time, that one would pity him; that upon a late reconciliation between him and the Duchess, after the quarrel they had had about the Mareschal de Brisac, he had given her a ring, and desired her to wear it; and that as she was dressing herself to come to the play, he had missed it on her finger, and asked what was become of it; upon which she seemed in surprise that she had it not, and called to her women for it, who unfortunately, or for want of being better instructed, made answer they had not seen it four or five days.

"It was," continued Monsieur d'Anville, "precisely so long, since the Mareschal de Brisac left the Court, and the King made no doubt but she gave him the ring when she took her leave of him. The thought of this awaked in so lively a manner that jealousy which was not yet extinguished, that he fell into uncommon transports, and loaded her with a thousand reproaches; he is just gone into her apartment again in great concern, but whether the reason is a more confirmed opinion that the Duchess had made a sacrifice of the ring, or for fear of having disobliged her by his anger, I can't tell.

"As soon as Monsieur d'Anville had told me this news, I acquainted Sancerre with it; I told it him as a secret newly entrusted with me, and charged him to say nothing of it.

"The next day I went early in the morning to my sister-in-law's, and found Madam de Tournon at her bedside, who had no great kindness for the Duchess of Valentinois, and knew very well that my sister-in-law had no reason to be satisfied with her. Sancerre had been with her, after he went from the play, and had acquainted her with the quarrel between the King and the Duchess; and Madam de Tournon was come to tell it to my sister-in-law, without knowing or suspecting that it was I from whom her lover had it.

"As soon as I advanced toward my sister-in-law, she told Madam de Tournon, that they might trust me with what she had been telling her; and without waiting Madam de Tournon's leave she related to me word by word all I had told Sancerre the night before. You may judge what surprise I was in; I looked hard at Madam de Tournon, and she seemed disordered; her disorder gave me a suspicion. I had told the thing to nobody but Sancerre; he left me when the comedy was done, without giving any reason for it; I remembered to have heard him speak much in praise of Madam de Tournon; all these things opened my eyes, and I easily discerned there was an intrigue between them, and that he had seen her since he left me.

"I was so stung to find he had concealed this adventure from me, that I said several things which made Madam de Tournon sensible of the imprudence she had been guilty of; I led her back to her coach, and assured her, I envied the happiness of him who informed her of the King's quarrel with the Duchess of Valentinois.

"I went immediately in search of Sancerre, and severely reproached him; I told him I knew of his passion for Madam de Tournon, without saying how I came by the discovery; he was forced to acknowledge it; I afterwards informed him what led me into the knowledge of it, and he acquainted me with the detail of the whole affair; he told me, that though he was a younger brother, and far from being able to pretend to so good a match, nevertheless she was determined to marry him. I can't express the surprise I was in; I told Sancerre he would do well to hasten the conclusion of the marriage, and that there was nothing he had not to fear from a woman who had the artifice to support, in the eye of the public, appearances so distant from truth; he gave me in answer that she was really concerned for the loss of her husband, but that the inclination she had for him had surmounted that affliction, and that she could not help discovering all on a sudden so great a change; he mentioned besides several other reasons in her excuse, which convinced me how desperately he was in love; he assured me he would bring her to consent that I should know his passion for her, especially since it was she herself who had made me suspect it; in a word, he did oblige her to it, though with a great deal of difficulty, and I grew afterwards very deep in their confidence.

"I never knew a lady behave herself in so genteel and agreeable a manner to her lover, but yet I was always shocked at the affectation she showed in appearing so concerned for the loss of her husband. Sancerre was so much in love, and so well pleased with the treatment he received from her, that he scarce durst press her to conclude the marriage, for fear she should think he desired it rather out of interest than love; however he spoke to her of it, and she seemed fully bent on marrying him; she began also to abandon her reserved manner of life, and to appear again in public; she visited my sister-in-law at hours when some of the Court were usually there; Sancerre came there but seldom, but those who came every night, and frequently saw her there, thought her extremely beautiful.

"She had not long quitted her solitude, when Sancerre imagined that her passion for him was cooled; he spoke of it several times to me: but I laid no great stress on the matter; but at last, when he told me, that instead of forwarding the marriage, she seemed to put it off, I began to think he was not to blame for being uneasy: I remonstrated to him, that if Madam de Tournon's passion was abated after having continued two years, he ought not to be surprised at it, and that even supposing it was not abated, possibly it might not be strong enough to induce her to marry him; that he ought not to complain of it; that such a marriage in the judgment of the public would draw censures upon her, not only because he was not a suitable match for her, but also on account of the prejudice it would do her reputation; that therefore all he could desire was, that she might not deceive him, nor lead him into false expectations; I told him further, that if she had not resolution enough to marry him, or if she confessed she liked some other person better, he ought not to resent or be angry at it, but still continue his esteem and regard for her.

"I give you," said I, "the advice which I would take myself; for sincerity has such charms to me, that I believe if my mistress, or even my wife ingenuously confessed, she had a greater affection for another than for me, I might be troubled, but not exasperated; I would lay aside the character of a lover or a husband, to bestow my advice and my pity."

This discourse made Madam de Cleves blush, and she found in it a certain similitude of her own condition, which very much surprised her, and gave her a concern, from which she could not recover in a great while.

"Sancerre spoke to Madam de Tournon," continued Monsieur de Cleves, "and told her all I had advised him; but she encouraged him with so many fresh assurances, and seemed so displeased at his suspicions, that she entirely removed them; nevertheless she deferred the marriage until after a pretty long journey he was to make; but she behaved herself so well until his departure, and appeared so concerned at it, that I believed as well as he, that she sincerely loved him. He set out about three months ago; during his absence I have seldom seen Madam de Tournon; you have entirely taken me up, and I only knew that he was speedily expected.

"The day before yesterday, on my arrival at Paris, I heard she was dead; I sent to his lodgings to enquire if they had any news of him, and word was brought me he came to town the night before, which was precisely the day that Madam de Tournon died; I immediately went to see him, concluding in what condition I should find him, but his affliction far surpassed what I had imagined.

"Never did I see a sorrow so deep and so tender; the moment he saw me he embraced me with tears; 'I shall never see her more,' said he, 'I shall never see her more, she is dead, I was not worthy of her, but I shall soon follow her.'

"After this he was silent; and then, from time to time, continually repeating 'She is dead, I shall never see her more,' he returned to lamentations and tears, and continued as a man bereft of reason. He told me he had not often received letters from her during his absence, but that he knew her too well to be surprised at it, and was sensible how shy and timorous she was of writing; he made no doubt but she would have married him upon his return; he considered her as the most amiable and constant of her sex; he thought himself tenderly beloved by her; he lost her the moment he expected to be united to her for ever; all these thoughts threw him into so violent an affliction, that I own I was deeply touched with it.

"Nevertheless I was obliged to leave him to go to the King, but promised to return immediately; accordingly I did, and I was never so surprised as I was to find him entirely changed from what I had left him; he was standing in his chamber, his face full of fury, sometimes walking, sometimes stopping short, as if he had been distracted; 'Come,' says he, 'and see the most forlorn wretch in the world; I am a thousand times more unhappy than I was a while ago, and what I have just heard of Madam de Tournon is worse than her death.'

"I took what he said to be wholly the effect of grief, and could not imagine that there could be anything worse than the death of a mistress one loves and is beloved by; I told him, that so far as he kept his grief within bounds, I approved of it, and bore a part in it; but that I should no longer pity him, if he abandoned himself to despair and flew from reason. 'I should be too happy if I had lost both my reason and my life,' cried he; 'Madam de Tournon was false to me, and I am informed of her unfaithfulness and treachery the very day after I was informed of her death; I am informed of it at a time when my soul is filled with the most tender love, and pierced with the sharpest grief that ever was; at a time when the

- 34 -

idea of her in my heart, is that of the most perfect woman who ever lived, and the most perfect with respect to me; I find I am mistaken, and that she does not deserve to be lamented by me; nevertheless I have the same concern for her death, as if she had been true to me, and I have the same sensibility of her falsehood, as if she were yet living; had I heard of her falsehood before her death, jealousy, anger, and rage would have possessed me, and in some measure hardened me against the grief for her loss; but now my condition is such, that I am incapable of receiving comfort, and yet know not how to hate her.'

"You may judge of the surprise I was in at what Sancerre told me; I asked him how he came by the knowledge of it, and he told me that the minute I went away from him, Etouteville, who is his intimate friend, but who nevertheless knew nothing of his love for Madam de Tournon, came to see him; that as soon as he was sat down, he fell a-weeping, and asked his pardon for having concealed from him what he was going to tell him, that he begged him to have compassion of him, that he was come to open his heart to him, and that he was the person in the world the most afflicted for the death of Madam de Tournon.

"'That name,' said Sancerre, 'so astonished me, that though my first intention was to tell him I was more afflicted than he, I had not the power to speak: he continued to inform me, that he had been in love with her six months, that he was always desirous to let me know it, but she had expressly forbid him; and in so authoritative a manner, that he durst not disobey her; that he gained her in a manner as soon as he courted her, that they concealed their mutual passion for each other from the whole world, that he never visited her publicly, that he had the pleasure to remove her sorrow for her husband's death, and that lastly he was to have married her at the very juncture in which she died; but that this marriage, which was an effect of love, would have appeared in her an effect of duty and obedience, she having prevailed upon her father to lay his commands on her to marry him, in order to avoid the appearance of too great an alteration in her conduct, which had seemed so averse to a second marriage.'

"'While Etouteville was speaking to me,' said Sancerre, 'I believed all he said, because I found so much probability in it, and because the time when he told me his passion for Madam de Tournon commenced, is precisely the same with that when she appeared changed towards me; but the next morning I thought him a liar, or at least an enthusiast, and was upon the point of telling him so. Afterwards I came into an inclination of clearing up the matter, and proposed several questions, and laid my doubts before him, in a word, I proceeded so far to convince myself of my misfortune, that he asked me if I knew Madam de Tournon's handwriting, and with that threw upon my bed four letters of hers and her picture; my brother came in that minute; Etouteville's face was so full of tears, that he was forced to withdraw to avoid being observed, and said he would come again in the evening to fetch what he left with me; and as for me, I sent my brother away under pretence of being indisposed, so impatient was I to see the letters he had left, and so full of hopes to find something there that might make me disbelieve what Etouteville had been telling me; but alas! What did I not find there? What tenderness! what assurances of marriage! what letters! She never wrote the like to me. Thus,' continued he, 'am I at once pierced with anguish for her death and for her falsehood, two evils which have been often compared, but never felt before by the same person at the same time; I confess, to my shame, that still I am more grieved for her loss than for her change; I cannot think her guilty enough, to consent to her death: were she living, I should have the satisfaction to reproach her, and to revenge myself on her by making her sensible of her injustice; but I shall see her no more, I shall see her no more; this is the greatest misfortune of all others; would I could restore her to life, though with the loss of my own! Yet what do I wish! If she were restored to life, she would live for Etouteville: how happy was I yesterday,' cried he, 'how happy! I was the most afflicted man in the world; but my affliction was reasonable, and there was something pleasing in the very thought that I was inconsolable; today all my sentiments are unjust; I pay to a feigned passion the tribute of my grief, which I thought I owed to a real one; I can neither hate nor love her memory; I am incapable of consolation, and yet don't know how to grieve for her; take care, I conjure you, that I never see Etouteville; his very name raises horror in me; I know very well I have no reason of complaint against him; I was to blame in concealing from him my love for Madam de Tournon; if he had known it, perhaps he would not have pursued her, perhaps she would not have been false to me; he came to me to impart his sorrows, and I cannot but pity him; alas! he had reason to love Madam de Tournon, he was beloved by her, and will never see her more: notwithstanding I perceive I can't help hating him; once more I conjure you take care I may not see him.'

"Sancerre burst afterwards into tears, began again to regret Madam de Tournon, and to speak to her, as if she were present, and say the softest things in the world; from these transports he passed to hatred, to complaints, to reproaches and imprecations against her. When I saw him in so desperate a condition, I found I should want somebody to assist me in appeasing his mind; accordingly I sent for his brother, whom I had left with the King; I met him in the anti-chamber, and acquainted him with Sancerre's condition: we gave the necessary orders to prevent his seeing Etouteville, and employed part of the night in endeavouring to make him capable of reason; this morning I found him yet more afflicted; his brother continued with him, and I returned to you."

"'Tis impossible to be more surprised than I am," said Madam de Cleves; "I thought Madam de Tournon equally incapable of love and falsehood." "Address and dissimulation," replied Monsieur de Cleves, "cannot go further than she carried them; observe, that when Sancerre thought her love to him was abated, it really was, and she began to love Etouteville; she told the last that he removed her sorrow for her husband's death, and that he was the cause of her quitting her retirement; Sancerre believed the cause was nothing but a resolution she had taken not to seem any longer to be in such deep affliction; she made a merit to Etouteville of concealing her correspondence with him, and of seeming forced to marry him by her father's command, as if it was an effect of the care she had of her reputation; whereas it was only an artifice to forsake Sancerre, without his having reason to resent it: I must return," continued Monsieur de Cleves, "to see this unhappy man, and I believe you would do well to go to Paris too; it is time for you to appear in the world again, and receive the numerous visits which you can't well dispense with."

Madam de Cleves agreed to the proposal, and returned to Paris the next day; she found herself much more easy with respect to the Duke de Nemours than she had been; what her mother had told her on her death-bed, and her grief for her death, created a sort of suspension in her mind as to her passion for the Duke, which made her believe it was quite effaced.

The evening of her arrival the Queen-Dauphin made her a visit, and after having condoled with her, told her that in order to divert her from melancholy thoughts, she would let her know all that had passed at Court in her absence; upon which she related to her a great many extraordinary things; "but what I have the greatest desire to inform you of," added she, "is that it is certain the Duke de Nemours is passionately in love; and that his most intimate friends are not only not entrusted in it, but can't so much as guess who the person is he is in love with; nevertheless this passion of his is so strong as to make him neglect, or to speak more properly, abandon the hopes of a Crown."

The Queen-Dauphin afterwards related whatever had passed in England; "What I have just told you," continued she, "I had from Monsieur d'Anville; and this morning he informed me, that last night the King sent for the Duke de Nemours upon the subject of Lignerol's letters, who desires to return, and wrote to his Majesty that he could no longer excuse to the Queen of England the Duke of Nemours's delay; that she begins to be displeased at it; and though she has not positively given her promise, she has said enough to encourage him to come over; the King showed this letter to the Duke of Nemours, who instead of speaking seriously as he had done at the beginning of this affair, only laughed and trifled, and made a jest of Lignerol's expectations: He said, 'The whole world would censure his imprudence, if he ventured to go to England, with the pretensions of marrying the Queen, without being secure of success; I think,' added he, 'I should time my business very ill to go to England now, when the King of Spain uses such pressing instances to obtain the Queen in marriage; the Spanish King perhaps would not be a very formidable rival in matters of gallantry, but in a treaty of marriage I believe your Majesty would not advise me to be his competitor.' 'I would advise you to it upon this occasion,' replied the King; 'but however you will have no competitor in him; I know he has quite other thoughts; and though he had not, Queen Mary found herself so uneasy under the weight of the Spanish Crown, that I can't believe her sister will be very desirous of it.' 'If she should not,' replied the Duke of Nemours, 'it is probable she will seek her happiness in love; she has been in love with my Lord Courtenay for several years; Queen Mary too was in love with him, and would have married him with consent of the states of her kingdom, had not she known that the youth and beauty of her sister Elizabeth had more charms for him than her crown; your Majesty knows, that the violence of her jealousy carried her so far, as to imprison them both, and afterwards to banish my Lord Courtenay, and at last determined her to marry the King of Spain; I believe Queen Elizabeth will soon recall that Lord, and make choice of a man whom she loves, who deserves her love, and who has suffered so much for her, in preference to another whom she never saw.' 'I should be of that opinion,' replied the King, 'if my Lord Courtenay were living, but I received advice some days ago, that he died at Padua, whither he was banished: I plainly see,' added the King, as he left the Duke, 'that your marriage must be concluded the same way the Dauphin's was, and that ambassadors must be sent to marry the Queen of England for you.'

"Monsieur d'Anville and the Viscount, who were with the King when he spoke to the Duke of Nemours, are persuaded that it is the passion he is so deeply engaged in, which diverts him from so great a design; the Viscount, who sees deeper into him than anybody, told Madam de Martigny that he was so changed he did not know him again; and what astonishes him more is, that he does not find he has any private interviews, or that he is ever missing at particular times, so that he believes he has no correspondence with the person he is in love with; and that which surprises him in the Duke is to see him in love with a woman who does not return his love."

What poison did this discourse of the Queen-Dauphin carry in it for Madam de Cleves? How could she but know herself to be the person whose name was not known, and how could she help being filled with tenderness and gratitude, when she learned, by a way not in the least liable to suspicion, that the Duke, who had already touched her heart, concealed his passion from the whole world, and neglected for her sake the hopes of a Crown? It is impossible to express what she felt, or to describe the tumult that was raised in her soul. Had the Queen-Dauphin observed her closely, she might easily have discerned, that what she had been saying was not indifferent to her; but as she had not the least suspicion of the truth, she continued her discourse without minding her: "Monsieur d'Anville," added she, "from whom, as I just told you, I had all this, believes I know more of it than himself, and he has so great an opinion of my beauty, that he is satisfied I am the only person capable of creating so great a change in the Duke of Nemours."

These last words of the Queen-Dauphin gave Madam de Cleves a sort of uneasiness very different from that which she had a few minutes before. "I can easily come into Monsieur d'Anville's opinion," answered she; "and 'tis very probable, Madam, that nothing less than a Princess of your merit could make him despise the Queen of England." "I would own it to you, if I knew it," replied the Queen-Dauphin, "and I should know it, if it were true; such passions as these never escape the sight of those who occasion them; they are the first to discern them; the Duke of Nemours has never showed me anything but slight complaisances; and yet I find so great a difference betwixt his present and former behaviour to me, that I can assure you, I am not the cause of the indifference he expresses for the Crown of England.

"But I forget myself in your company," added the Queen-Dauphin, "and don't remember that I am to wait upon Madame: you know the peace is as good as concluded, but perhaps you don't know that the King of Spain has refused to sign it, but on condition of marrying this Princess, instead of the Prince Don Carlos, his son: the King was with great difficulty brought to allow it, but at last he has consented, and is gone to carry the news to Madame; I believe she will be inconsolable. To marry a man of the King of Spain's age and temper can never be pleasing, especially to her who has all the gaiety which the bloom of youth joined with beauty inspires, and was in expectation of marrying a young Prince for whom she has an inclination without having seen him. I do not know whether the King will find in her all the obedience he desires; he has charged me to see her, because he knows she loves me, and believes I shall be able to influence her. From thence I shall make a visit of a very different nature, to congratulate the King's sister. All things are ready for her marriage with the Prince of Savoy, who is expected in a few days. Never was a woman of her age so entirely pleased to be married; the Court will be more numerous and splendid than ever, and notwithstanding your grief, you must come among us, in order to make strangers see that we are furnished with no mean beauties."

Having said this, the Queen-Dauphin took her leave of Madam de Cleves, and the next day Madame's marriage was publicly known; some days after the King and the Queens went to visit the Princess of Cleves; the Duke de Nemours, who had expected her return with the utmost impatience, and languished for an opportunity of speaking to her in private, contrived to wait upon her at an hour, when the company would probably be withdrawing, and nobody else come in; he succeeded in his design, and came in when the last visitors were going away.

The Princess was sitting on her bed, and the hot weather, together with the sight of the Duke de Nemours, gave her a blush that added to her beauty; he sat over against her with a certain timorous respect, that flows from a real love; he continued some minutes without speaking; nor was she the less at a loss, so that they were both silent a good while: at last the Duke condoled with her for her mother's death; Madam de Cleves was glad to give the conversation that turn, spoke a considerable time of the great loss she had had, and at last said, that though time had taken off from the violence of her grief, yet the impression would always remain so strong, that it would entirely change her humour. "Great troubles and excessive passions," replied the Duke, "make great alterations in the mind; as for me, I am quite another man since my return from Flanders; abundance of people have taken notice of this change, and the Queen-Dauphin herself spoke to me of it yesterday." "It is true," replied the Princess, "she has observed it, and I think I remember to have heard her say something about it." "I'm not sorry, Madam," replied the Duke, "that she has discerned it, but I could wish some others in particular had discerned it too; there are persons to whom we dare give no other evidences of the passion we have for them, but by things which do not concern them; and when we dare not let them know we love them, we should be glad at least to have them see we are not desirous of being loved by any other; we should be glad to convince them, that no other beauty, though of the highest rank, has any charms for us, and that a Crown would be too dear, if purchased with no less a price than absence from her we adore: women ordinarily," continued he, "judge of the passion one has for them, by the care one takes to oblige, and to be assiduous about them; but it's no hard matter to do this, though they be ever so little amiable; not to give oneself up to the pleasure of pursuing them, to shun them through fear of discovering to the public, and in a manner to themselves, the sentiments one has for them, here lies the difficulty; and what still more demonstrates the truth of one's passion is, the becoming entirely changed from what one was, and the having no longer a gust either for ambition or pleasure, after one has employed one's whole life in pursuit of both."

The Princess of Cleves readily apprehended how far she was concerned in this discourse; one while she seemed of opinion that she ought not to suffer such an address; another, she thought she ought not to seem to understand it, or show she supposed herself meant by it; she thought she ought to speak, and she thought she ought to be silent; the Duke of Nemours's discourse equally pleased and offended her; she was convinced by it of the truth of all the Queen-Dauphin had led her to think; she found in it somewhat gallant and respectful, but also somewhat bold and too intelligible; the inclination she had for the Duke gave her an anxiety which it was not in her power to control; the most obscure expressions of a man that pleases, move more than the most open declaration of one we have no liking for; she made no answer; the Duke de Nemours took notice of her silence, which perhaps would have proved no ill-presage, if the coming in of the Prince of Cleves had not ended at once the conversation and the visit.

The Prince was coming to give his wife a further account of Sancerre, but she was not over curious to learn the sequel of that adventure; she was so much taken up with what had just passed, that she could hardly conceal the embarrassment she was in. When she was at liberty to muse upon it, she plainly saw she was mistaken, when she thought she was indifferent as to the Duke de Nemours; what he had said to her had made all the impression he could desire, and had entirely convinced her of his passion; besides the Duke's actions agreed too well with his words to leave her the least doubt about it; she no longer flattered herself that she did not love him; all her care was not to let him discover it, a task of which she had already experienced the difficulty; she knew the only way to succeed in it was to avoid seeing him; and as her mourning gave her an excuse for being more retired than usual, she made use of that pretence not to go to places where he might see her; she was full of melancholy; her mother's death was the seeming cause of it, and no suspicion was had of any other.

The Duke de Nemours, not seeing her any more, fell into desperation and knowing he should not meet with her in any public assembly, or at any diversions the Court joined in, he could not prevail upon himself to appear there, and therefore he pretended a great love for hunting, and made matches for that sport on the days when the Queens kept their assemblies; a slight indisposition had served him a good while as an excuse for staying at home, and declining to go to places where he knew very well that Madam de Cleves would not be.

The Prince of Cleves was ill almost at the same time, and the Princess never stirred out of his room during his illness; but when he grew better, and received company, and among others the Duke de Nemours, who under pretence of being yet weak, stayed with him the greatest part of the day, she found she could not continue any longer there; and yet in the first visits he made she had not the resolution to go out; she had been too long without seeing him, to be able to resolve to see him no more; the Duke had the address, by discourses that appeared altogether general, but which she understood very well by the relation they had to what he had said privately to her, to let her know that he went a-hunting only to be more at liberty to think of her, and that the reason of his not going to the assemblies was her not being there.

At last she executed the resolution she had taken to go out of her husband's room, whenever he was there, though this was doing the utmost violence to herself: the Duke perceived she avoided him, and the thought of it touched him to the heart.

The Prince of Cleves did not immediately take notice of his wife's conduct in this particular, but at last he perceived she went out of the room when there was company there; he spoke to her of it, and she told him that she did not think it consistent with decency to be every evening among the gay young courtiers; that she hoped he would allow her to live in a more reserved manner than she had done hitherto, that the virtue and presence of her mother authorised her in many liberties which could not otherwise be justified in a woman of her age.

Monsieur de Cleves, who had a great deal of facility and complaisance for his wife, did not show it on this occasion, but told her he would by no means consent to her altering her conduct; she was upon the point of telling him, it was reported that the Duke de Nemours was in love with her, but she had not the power to name him; besides she thought it disingenuous to disguise the truth, and make use of pretences to a man who had so good an opinion of her.

Some days after the King was with the Queen at the assembly hour, and the discourse turned upon nativities and predictions; the company were divided in their opinion as to what credit ought to be given to them; the Queen professed to have great faith in them, and maintained that after so many things had come to pass as they had been foretold, one could not doubt but there was something of certainty in that science; others affirmed, that of an infinite number of predictions so very few proved true, that the truth of those few ought to be looked upon as an effect of chance.

"I have formerly been very curious and inquisitive as to futurity," said the King, "but I have seen so many false and improbable things, that I am satisfied there is no truth in that pretended art. Not many years since there came hither a man of great reputation in astrology; everybody went to see him; I went among others, but without saying who I was, and I carried with me the Duke of Guise and Descars, and made them go in first; nevertheless the astrologer addressed himself first to me, as if he had concluded me to be their master; perhaps he knew me, and yet he told me one thing that was very unsuitable to my character, if he had known me; his prediction was that I should be killed in a duel; he told the Duke of Guise, that he should die of a wound received behind; and he told Descars he should be knocked of the head by the kick of a horse; the Duke of Guise was a little angry at the prediction, as if it imported he should run away; nor was Descars better pleased to find he was to make his exit by so unfortunate an accident; in a word, we went away all three of us very much out of humour with the astrologer; I don't know what will happen to the Duke of Guise and Descars, but there is not much probability of my being killed in a duel; the King of Spain and I have just made peace, and if we had not, I question whether we should have fought, or if I should have challenged him, as the King my father did Charles the Fifth."

After the King had related the misfortune that was foretold him, those who had defended astrology abandoned the argument, and agreed there was no credit to be given to it: "For my part," said the Duke de Nemours aloud, "I have the least reason of any man in the world to credit it"; and then turning himself to Madam de Cleves, near whom he stood, "it has been foretold me," says he very softly, "that I should be happy in a person for whom I should have the most violent and respectful passion; you may judge, Madam, if I ought to believe in predictions."

The Queen-Dauphin, who believed, from what the Duke had spoke aloud, that what he whispered was some false prediction that had been told him, asked him what it was he said to Madam de Cleves; had he had a less ready wit, he would have been surprised at this question; but without any hesitation, "What I said to her, Madam," answered he, "was, that it had been predicted to me, that I should be raised to a higher fortune than my most sanguine hopes could lead me to expect." "If nothing have been foretold you but this," replied the Queen-Dauphin, smiling, and thinking of the affair of England, "I would not advise you to decry astrology; you may have reasons hereafter to offer in defence of it." Madam de Cleves apprehended the Queen-Dauphin's meaning, but knew withal, that the fortune the Duke of Nemours spoke of was not that of being King of England.

The time of her mourning being expired, the Princess of Cleves was obliged to make her appearance again, and go to Court as usual; she saw the Duke de Nemours at the Queen-Dauphin's apartment; she saw him at the Prince of Cleves's, where he often came in company of other young noblemen, to avoid being remarked; yet she never once saw him, but it gave her a pain that could not escape his observation.

However industrious she was to avoid being looked at by him, and to speak less to him than to any other, some things escaped her in an unguarded moment, which convinced him he was not indifferent to her; a man of less discernment than he would not have perceived it, but he had already so often been the object of love, that it was easy for him to know when he was loved; he found the Chevalier de Guise was his rival, and the Chevalier knew that the Duke de Nemours was his; Monsieur de Guise was the only man in the Court that had unravelled this affair, his interest having made him more clear-sighted than others; the knowledge they had of each other's sentiments created an opposition between them in everything, which, however, did not break out into an open quarrel; they were always of different parties at the running, at the ring, at tournaments, and all diversions the King delighted in, and their emulation was so great it could not be concealed.

Madam de Cleves frequently revolved in her mind the affair of England; she believed the Duke de Nemours could not resist the advice of the King, and the instances of Lignerolles; she was very much concerned to find that Lignerolles was not yet returned, and she impatiently expected him; her inclinations strongly swayed her to inform herself exactly of the state of this affair; but the same reasons, which raised in her that curiosity, obliged her to conceal it, and she only enquired of the beauty, the wit, and the temper of Queen Elizabeth. A picture of that Princess had been brought the King, which Madam de Cleves found much handsomer than she could have wished for, and she could not forbear saying, the picture flattered. "I don't think so," replied the Queen-Dauphin; "that Princess has the reputation of being very handsome, and of having a very exalted genius, and I know she has always been proposed to me as a model worthy my imitation; she can't but be very handsome, if she resembles her mother, Anne Boleyn; never had woman so many charms and allurements both in her person and her humour; I have heard say she had something remarkably lively in her countenance, very different from what is usually found in other English beauties." "I think," replied Madam de Cleves, "'tis said she was born in France." "Those who imagine so are mistaken," replied the Queen-Dauphin; "I'll give you her history in a few words.

"She was of a good family in England; Henry the Eighth was in love with her sister and her mother, and it has been even suspected by some, that she was his daughter; she came to France with Henry the Seventh's sister, who married Louis XII that Princess, who was full of youth and gallantry, left the Court of France with great reluctance after her husband's death; but Anne Boleyn, who had the same inclinations as her mistress, could not prevail with herself to go away; the late King was in love with her, and she continued maid of honour to Queen Claude; that Queen died, and Margaretta, the King's sister, Duchess of Alenson, and since Queen of Navarre, whose story you know, took her into her service, where she imbibed the principles of the new religion; she returned afterwards to England, and there charmed all the world; she had the manners of France, which please in all countries; she sung well, she danced finely; she was a maid of honour to Queen Catherine, and Henry the Eighth fell desperately in love with her.

"Cardinal Wolsey, his favourite and first minister, being dissatisfied with the Emperor for not having favoured his pretensions to the Papacy, in order to revenge himself of him, contrived an alliance between France and the King his master; he put it into the head of Henry the Eighth, that his marriage with the Emperor's aunt was null, and advised him to marry the Duchess of Alenson, whose husband was just dead; Anne Boleyn, who was not without ambition, considered Queen Catherine's divorce as a means that would bring her to the Crown; she began to give the King of England impressions of the Lutheran religion, and engaged the late King to favour at Rome Henry the Eighth's divorce, in hopes of his marrying the Duchess of Alenson; Cardinal Wolsey, that he might have an opportunity of treating this affair, procured himself to be sent to France upon other pretences; but his master was so far from permitting him to propose this marriage, that he sent him express orders to Calais not to speak of it.

"Cardinal Wolsey, at his return from France, was received with as great honours as could have been paid to the King himself; never did any favourite carry his pride and vanity to so great a height; he managed an interview between the two Kings at Boulogne, when Francis the First would have given the upperhand to Henry the Eighth, but he refused to accept it; they treated one another by turns with the utmost magnificence, and presented to each habits of the same sort with those they wore themselves. I remember to have heard say, that those the late King sent to the King of England were of crimson satin beset all over with pearls and diamonds, and a robe of white velvet embroidered with gold; after having stayed some time at Boulogne, they went to Calais. Anne Boleyn was lodged in Henry the Eighth's Court with the train of a Queen; and Francis the First made her the same presents, and paid her the same honours as if she had been really so: in a word, after a passion of nine year's continuance King Henry married her, without waiting for the dissolving of his first marriage. The Pope precipitately thundered out excommunications against him, which so provoked King Henry, that he declared himself head of the Church, and drew after him all England into the unhappy change in which you see it.

"Anne Boleyn did not long enjoy her greatness; for when she thought herself most secure of it by the death of Queen Catherine, one day as she was seeing a match of running at the ring made by the Viscount Rochefort her brother, the King was struck with such a jealousy, that he abruptly left the show, went away to London, and gave orders for arresting the Queen, the Viscount Rochefort, and several others whom he believed to be the lovers or confidants of that Princess. Though this jealousy in appearance had its birth that moment, the King had been long possessed with it by the Viscountess Rochefort, who not being able to bear the strict intimacy between her husband and the Queen, represented it to the King as a criminal commerce; so that that Prince, who was besides in love with Jane Seymour, thought of nothing but ridding himself of Anne Boleyn; and in less than three weeks he caused the Queen and her brother to be tried, had them both beheaded, and, married Jane Seymour. He had afterwards several wives, whom he divorced or put to death; and among others Catherine Howard, whose confidant the Viscountess Rochefort was, and who was beheaded with her: thus was she punished for having falsely accused Anne Boleyn. And Henry the Eighth died, being become excessive fat."

All the ladies, that were present when the Queen-Dauphin made this relation, thanked her for having given them so good an account of the Court of England; and among the rest Madam de Cleves, who could not forbear asking several questions concerning Queen Elizabeth.

The Queen-Dauphin caused pictures in miniature to be drawn of all the beauties of the Court, in order to send them to the Queen her mother. One day, when that of Madam de Cleves was finishing, the Queen-Dauphin came to spend the afternoon with her; the Duke de Nemours did not fail to be there; he let slip no opportunities of seeing Madam de Cleves, yet without appearing to contrive them. She looked so pretty that day, that he would have fell in love with her, though he had not been so before: however he durst not keep his eyes fixed upon her, while she was sitting for her picture, for fear of showing too much the pleasure he took in looking at her.

The Queen-Dauphin asked Monsieur de Cleves for a little picture he had of his wife's, to compare it with that which was just drawn; everybody gave their judgment of the one and the other; and Madam de Cleves ordered the painter to mend something in the headdress of that which had been just brought in; the painter in obedience to her took the picture out of the case in which it was, and having mended it laid it again on the table.

The Duke de Nemours had long wished to have a picture of Madam de Cleves; when he saw that which Monsieur de Cleves had, he could not resist the temptation of stealing it from a husband, who, he believed, was tenderly loved; and he thought that among so many persons as were in the same room he should be no more liable to suspicion than another.

The Queen-Dauphin was sitting on the bed, and whispering to Madam de Cleves, who was standing before her. Madam de Cleves, through one of the curtains that was but half-drawn, spied the Duke de Nemours with his back to the table, that stood at the bed's feet, and perceived that without turning his face he took something very dextrously from off the table; she presently guessed it was her picture, and was in such concern about it, that the Queen-Dauphin observed she did not attend to what she said, and asked her aloud what it was she looked at. At those words, the Duke de Nemours turned about, and met full the eyes of Madam de Cleves that were still fixed upon him; he thought it not impossible but she might have seen what he had done.

Madam de Cleves was not a little perplexed; it was reasonable to demand her picture of him; but to demand it publicly was to discover to the whole world the sentiments which the Duke had for her, and to demand it in private would be to engage him to speak of his love; she judged after all it was better to let him keep it, and she was glad to grant him a favour which she could do without his knowing that she granted it. The Duke de Nemours, who observed her perplexity, and partly guessed the cause of it, came up, and told her softly, "If you have seen what I have ventured to do, be so good, Madam, as to let me believe you are ignorant of it; I dare ask no more"; having said this he withdrew, without waiting for her answer.

The Queen-Dauphin went to take a walk, attended with the rest of the ladies; and the Duke de Nemours went home to shut himself up in his closet, not being able to support in public the ecstasy he was in on having a picture of Madam de Cleves; he tasted everything that was sweet in love; he was in love with the finest woman of the Court; he found she loved him against her will, and saw in all her actions that sort of care and embarrassment which love produces in young and innocent hearts.

At night great search was made for the picture; and having found the case it used to be kept in, they never suspected it had been stolen but thought it might have fallen out by chance. The Prince of Cleves was very much concerned for the loss of it; and after having searched for it a great while to no purpose, he told his wife, but with an air that showed he did not think so, that without doubt she had some secret lover, to whom she had given the picture, or who had stole it, and that none but a lover would have been contented with the picture without the case.

These words, though spoke in jest, made a lively impression in the mind of Madam de Cleves; they gave her remorse, and she reflected on the violence of her inclination which hurried her on to love the Duke of

Nemours; she found she was no longer mistress of her words or countenance; she imagined that Lignerolles was returned, that she had nothing to fear from the affair of England, nor any cause to suspect the Queen-Dauphin; in a word, that she had no refuge or defence against the Duke de Nemours but by retiring; but as she was not at her liberty to retire, she found herself in a very great extremity and ready to fall into the last misfortune, that of discovering to the Duke the inclination she had for him: she remembered all that her mother had said to her on her death-bed, and the advice which she gave her, to enter on any resolutions, however difficult they might be, rather than engage in gallantry; she remembered also what Monsieur de Cleves had told her, when he gave an account of Madam de Tournon; she thought she ought to acknowledge to him the inclination she had for the Duke de Nemours, and in that thought she continued a long time; afterwards she was astonished to have entertained so ridiculous a design, and fell back again into her former perplexity of not knowing what to choose.

The peace was signed; and the Lady Elizabeth, after a great deal of reluctance, resolved to obey the King her father. The Duke of Alva was appointed to marry her in the name of the Catholic King, and was very soon expected. The Duke of Savoy too, who was to marry the King's sister, and whose nuptials were to be solemnised at the same time, was expected every day. The King thought of nothing but how to grace these marriages with such diversions as might display the politeness and magnificence of his Court. Interludes and comedies of the best kind were proposed, but the King thought those entertainments too private, and desired to have somewhat of a more splendid nature: he resolved to make a solemn tournament, to which strangers might be invited, and of which the people might be spectators. The princes and young lords very much approved the King's design, especially the Duke of Ferrara, Monsieur de Guise, and the Duke de Nemours, who surpassed the rest in these sorts of exercises. The King made choice of them to be together with himself the four champions of the tournament.

Proclamation was made throughout the kingdom, that on the 15th of June in the City of Paris, his most Christian Majesty, and the Princes Alphonso d'Ete Duke of Ferrara, Francis of Loraine Duke of Guise, and James of Savoy Duke of Nemours would hold an open tournament against all comers. The first combat to be on horse-back in the lists, with double armour, to break four lances, and one for the ladies; the second combat with swords, one to one, or two to two, as the judges of the field should direct; the third combat on foot, three pushes of pikes, and six hits with the sword. The champions to furnish lances, swords, and pikes, at the choice of the combatants. Whoever did not manage his horse in the carreer to be put out of the lists; four judges of the field to give orders. The combatants who should break most lances and perform best to carry the prize, the value whereof to be at the discretion of the judges; all the combatants, as well French as strangers, to be obliged to touch one or more, at their choice, of the shields that should hang on the pillar at the end of the lists, where a herald at arms should be ready to receive them, and enroll them according to their quality, and the shields they had touched; the combatants to be obliged to cause their shields and arms to be brought by a gentleman and hung up at the pillar three days before the tournament, otherwise not to be admitted without leave of the champions.

A spacious list was made near the Bastille, which begun from the Chateau des Tournelles and crossed the street of St. Anthony, and extended as far as the King's stables; on both sides were built scaffolds and amphitheatres, which formed a sort of galleries that made a very fine sight, and were capable of containing an infinite number of people. The princes and lords were wholly taken up in providing what was necessary for a splendid appearance, and in mingling in their cyphers and devices somewhat of gallantry that had relation to the ladies they were in love with.

A few days before the Duke of Alva's arrival, the King made a match at tennis with the Duke de Nemours, the Chevalier de Guise, and the Viscount de Chartres. The Queens came to see them play, attended with the ladies of the Court, and among others Madam de Cleves. After the game was ended, as they went out of the tennis court, Chatelart came up to the Queen-Dauphin, and told her fortune had put into his hands a letter of gallantry, that dropped out of the Duke de Nemours's pocket. This Queen, who was always very curious in what related to the Duke, bid Chatelart give her the letter; he did so, and she followed the Queen her mother-in-law, who was going with the King to see them work at the lists. After they had been there some time, the King caused some horses to be brought that had been lately taken in, and though they were not as yet thoroughly managed, he was for mounting one of them, and ordered his attendants to mount others; the King and the Duke de Nemours hit upon the most fiery and high mettled of them. The horses were ready to fall foul on one another, when the Duke of Nemours, for fear of hurting the King, retreated abruptly, and ran back his horse against a pillar with so much violence that the shock of it made him stagger. The company ran up to him, and he was thought considerably hurt; but the Princess of Cleves thought the hurt much greater than anyone else. The interest she had in it gave her an apprehension and concern which she took no care to conceal; she came up to him with the Queens, and with a countenance so changed, that one less concerned than the Chevalier de Guise might have perceived it: perceive it he immediately did, and was much more intent upon the condition Madam de Cleves was in, than upon that of the Duke de Nemours. The blow the Duke had given himself had so stunned him, that he continued some time leaning his head on those who supported him; when he raised himself up, he immediately viewed Madam de Cleves, and saw in her face the concern she was in for him, and he looked upon her in a manner which made her sense how much he was touched with it: afterwards he thanked the Queens for the goodness they had expressed to him, and made apologies for the condition he had been in before them; and then the King ordered him to go to rest.

Madam de Cleves, after she was recovered from the fright she had been in, presently reflected on the tokens she had given of it. The Chevalier de Guise did not suffer her to continue long in the hope that nobody had perceived it, but giving her his hand to lead her out of the lists: "I have more cause to complain, Madam," said he, "than the Duke de Nemours; pardon me, if I forget for a moment that profound respect I have always had for you, and show you how much my heart is grieved for what my eyes have just seen; this is the first time I have ever been so bold as to speak to you, and it will be the last. Death or at least eternal absence will remove me from a place where I can live no longer, since I have now lost the melancholy comfort I had of believing that all who behold you with love are as unhappy as myself."

Madam de Cleves made only a confused answer, as if she had not understood what the Chevalier's words meant: at another time she would have been offended if he had mentioned the passion he had for her; but at this moment she felt nothing but the affliction to know that he had observed the passion she had for the Duke de Nemours. The Chevalier de Guise was so well convinced of it, and so pierced with grief, that from that moment he took a resolution never to think of being loved by Madam de Cleves; but that he might the better be able to quit a passion which he had thought so difficult and so glorious, it was necessary to make choice of some other undertaking worthy of employing him; he had his view on Rhodes: the taking of which he had formerly had some idea of; and when death snatched him away, in the flower of his youth, and at a time when he had acquired the reputation of one of the greatest Princes of his age, the only regret he had to part with life was, that he had not been able to execute so noble a resolution, the success whereof he thought infallible from the great care he had taken about it.

Madam de Cleves, when she came out of the lists, went to the Queen's apartment, with her thoughts wholly taken up with what had passed. The Duke de Nemours came there soon after, richly dressed, and like one wholly unsensible of the accident that had befallen him; he appeared even more gay than usual, and the joy he was in for what he had discovered, gave him an air that very much increased his natural agreeableness. The whole Court was surprised when he came in; and there was nobody but asked him how he did, except Madam de Cleves, who stayed near the chimney pretending not to see him. The King coming out of his closet, and seeing him among others called him to talk to him about his late accident. The Duke passed by Madam de Cleves, and said softly to her, "Madam, I have received this day some marks of your pity, but they were not such as I am most worthy of." Madam de Cleves suspected that he had taken notice of the concern she had been in for him, and what he now said convinced her she was not mistaken; it gave her a great deal of concern to find she was so little mistress of herself as not to have been able to conceal her inclinations from the Chevalier de Guise; nor was she the less concerned to see that the Duke de Nemours was acquainted with them; yet this last grief was not so entire, but there was a certain mixture of pleasure in it.

The Queen-Dauphin, who was extremely impatient to know what there was in the letter which Chatelart had given her, came up to Madam de Cleves. "Go read this letter," says she; "'tis addressed to the Duke de Nemours, and was probably sent him by the mistress for whom he has forsaken all others; if you can't read it now, keep it, and bring it me about bedtime and inform me if you know the hand." Having said this, the Queen-Dauphin went away from Madam de Cleves, and left her in such astonishment, that she was not able for some time to stir out of the place. The impatience and grief she was in not permitting her to stay at Court, she went home before her usual hour of retirement; she trembled with the letter in her hand, her thoughts were full of confusion, and she experienced I know not what of insupportable grief, that she had never felt before. No sooner was she in her closet, but she opened the letter and found it as follows:

> I have loved you too well to leave you in a belief that the change you observe in me is an effect of lightness; I must inform you that your falsehood is the cause of it; you will be surprised to hear me speak of your falsehood; you have dissembled it with so much skill, and I have taken so much care to conceal my knowledge of it from you, that you have reason to be surprised at the discovery; I am myself in wonder, that I have discovered nothing of it to you before; never was grief equal to mine; I thought you had the most violent passion for me, I did not conceal that

which I had for you, and at the time that I acknowledged it to you without reserve, I found that you deceived me, that you loved another, and that in all probability I was made a sacrifice to this new mistress. I knew it the day you run at the ring, and this was the reason I was not there; at first I pretended an indisposition in order to conceal my sorrow, but afterwards I really fell into one, nor could a constitution delicate like mine support so violent a shock. When I began to be better, I still counterfeited sickness, that I might have an excuse for not seeing and for not writing to you; besides I was willing to have time to come to a resolution in what manner to deal with you; I took and quitted the same resolution twenty times; but at last I concluded you deserved not to see my grief, and I resolved not to show you the least mark of it. I had a desire to bring down your pride, by letting you see, that my passion for you declined of itself: I thought I should by this lessen the value of the sacrifice you had made of me, and was loth you should have the pleasure of appearing more amiable in the eyes of another, by showing her how much I loved you; I resolved to write to you in a cold and languishing manner, that she, to whom you gave my letters, might perceive my love was at an end: I was unwilling she should have the satisfaction of knowing I was sensible that she triumphed over me, or that she should increase her triumph by my despair and complaints. I thought I should punish you too little by merely breaking with you, and that my ceasing to love you would give you but a slight concern, after you had first forsaken me; I found it was necessary you should love me, to feel the smart of not being loved, which I so severely experienced myself; I was of opinion that if anything could rekindle that flame, it would be to let you see that mine was extinguished, but to let you see it through an endeavour to conceal it from you, as if I wanted the power to acknowledge it to you: this resolution I adhered to; I found it difficult to take, and when I saw you again I thought it impossible to execute. I was ready a hundred times to break out into tears and complaints; my ill state of health, which still continued, served as a disguise to hide from you the affliction and trouble I was in; afterward I was supported by the pleasure of dissembling with you, as you had done with me; however it was doing so apparent a violence to myself to tell you or to write to you that I loved you, that you immediately perceived I had no mind to let you see my affection was altered; you was touched with this, you complained of it; I endeavoured to remove your fears, but it was done in so forced a manner, that you were still more convinced by it, I no longer loved you; in short, I did all I intended to do. The fantasticalness of your heart was such, that you advanced towards me in proportion as you saw I retreated from you. I have enjoyed all the pleasure which can arise from revenge; I plainly saw, that you loved me more than you had ever done, and I showed you I had no longer any love for you. I had even reason to believe that you had entirely abandoned her, for whom you had forsaken me; I had ground too to be satisfied you had never spoken to her concerning me; but neither your discretion in that particular, nor the return of your affection can make amends for your inconstancy; your heart has been divided between me and another, and you have deceived me; this is sufficient wholly to take from me the pleasure I found in being loved by you, as I thought I deserved to be, and to confirm me in the resolution I have taken never to see you more, which you are so much surprised at.

Madam de Cleves read this letter, and read it over again several times, without knowing at the same time what she had read; she saw only that the Duke de Nemours did not love her as she imagined and that he loved others who were no less deceived by him than she. What a discovery was this for a person in her condition, who had a violent passion, who had just given marks of it to a man whom she judged unworthy of it, and to another whom she used ill for his sake! Never was affliction so cutting as hers; she imputed the piercingness of it to what had happened that day, and believed that if the Duke de Nemours had not had ground to believe she loved him she should not have cared whether he loved another or not; but she deceived herself, and this evil which she found so insupportable was jealousy with all the horrors it can be accompanied with. This letter discovered to her a piece of gallantry the Duke de Nemours had been long engaged in; she saw the lady who wrote it was a person of wit and merit, and deserved to be loved; she found she had more courage than herself, and envied her the power she had had of concealing her sentiments from the Duke de Nemours; by the close of the letter, she saw this lady thought herself beloved, and presently suspected that the discretion the Duke had showed in his addresses to her, and which she had been so much taken with, was only an effect of his passion for this other mistress, whom he was afraid of disobliging; in short, she thought of everything that could add to her grief and despair. What reflections did she not make on herself, and on the advices her mother had given her I how did she repent, that she had not persisted in her resolution of retiring, though against the will of Monsieur de Cleves, or that she had not pursued her intentions of acknowledging to him the inclination she had for the Duke of Nemours! She was convinced, she would have done better to discover it to a husband, whose goodness she was sensible of, and whose interest it would have been to conceal it, than to let it appear to a man who was unworthy of it, who deceived her, who perhaps made a sacrifice of her, and who had no view in being loved by her but to gratify his pride and vanity; in a word, she found, that all the calamities that could befall her, and all the extremities she could be reduced to, were less than that single one of having discovered to the Duke de Nemours that she loved him, and of knowing that he loved another: all her comfort was to think, that after the knowledge of this she had nothing more to fear from herself, and that she should be entirely eased of the inclination she had for the Duke.

She never thought of the orders the Queen-Dauphin had given her, to come to her when she went to rest: she went to bed herself, and pretended to be ill; so that when Monsieur de Cleves came home from the King, they told him she was asleep. But she was far from that tranquillity which inclines to sleep; all the night she did nothing but torment herself, and read over and over the letter in her hand.

Madam de Cleves was not the only person whom this letter disturbed. The Viscount de Chartres, who had lost it and not the Duke de Nemours, was in the utmost inquietude about it. He had been that evening with the Duke of Guise, who had given a great entertainment to the Duke of Ferrara his brother-in-law, and to all the young people of the Court: it happened that the discourse turned upon ingenious letters; and the Viscount de Chartres said he had one about him the finest that ever was writ: they urged him to show it, and on his excusing himself, the Duke de Nemours insisted he had no such letter, and that what he said was only out of vanity; the Viscount made him answer, that he urged his discretion to the utmost, that nevertheless he would not show the letter; but he would read some parts of it, which would make it appear few men received the like. Having said this, he would have taken out the letter, but could not find it; he searched for it to no purpose. The company rallied him about it; but he seemed so disturbed, that they forbore to speak further of it; he withdrew sooner than the others, and went home with great impatience, to see if he had not left the letter there. While he was looking for it, one of the Queen's pages came to tell him, that the Viscountess d'Usez had thought it necessary to give him speedy advice, that it was said at the Queen's Court, that he had dropped a letter of gallantry out of his pocket while he was playing at tennis; that great part of what the letter contained had been related, that the Queen had expressed a great curiosity to see it, and had sent to one of her gentlemen for it, but that he answered, he had given it to Chatelart.

The page added many other particulars which heightened the Viscount's concern; he went out that minute to go to a gentleman who was an intimate friend of Chatelart's; and though it was a very unseasonable hour, made him get out of bed to go and fetch the letter, without letting him know who it was had sent for it, or who had lost it. Chatelart, who was prepossessed with an opinion that it belonged to the Duke of Nemours, and that the Duke was in love with the Queen-Dauphin, did not doubt but it was he who had sent to redemand it, and so answered with a malicious sort of joy, that he had put the letter into the Queen-Dauphin's hands. The gentleman brought this answer back to the Viscount de Chartres, which increased the uneasiness he was under already, and added new vexations to it: after having continued some time in an irresolution what to do, he found that the Duke de Nemours was the only person whose assistance could draw him out of this intricate affair.

Accordingly he went to the Duke's house, and entered his room about break of day. What the Duke had discovered the day before with respect to the Princess of Cleves had given him such agreeable ideas, that he slept very sweetly; he was very much surprised to find himself waked by the Viscount de Chartres, and asked him if he came to disturb his rest so early, to be revenged of him for what he had said last night at supper. The Viscount's looks soon convinced him, that he came upon a serious business; "I am come," said he, "to entrust you with the most important affair of my life; I know very well, you are not obliged to me for the confidence I place in you, because I do it at a time when I stand in need of your assistance; but I know likewise, that I should have lost your esteem, if I had acquainted you with all I am now going to tell you, without having been forced to it by absolute necessity: I have dropped the letter I spoke of last night; it is of the greatest consequence to me, that nobody should know it is addressed to me; it has been seen by abundance of people, who were at the tennis court yesterday when I dropped it; you was there too, and the favour I have to ask you, is, to say it was you who lost it." "Sure you think," replied the Duke de Nemours smiling, "that I have no mistress, by making such a proposal, and that I have no quarrels or inconveniences to apprehend by leaving it to be believed that I receive such letters." "I beg you," said the Viscount, "to hear me seriously; if you have a mistress, as I doubt not you have, though I do not know who she is, it will be easy for you to justify yourself, and I'll put you into an infallible way of doing it. As for you, though you should fail in justifying yourself, it can cost you nothing but a short falling out; but for my part, this accident affects me in a very different manner, I shall dishonour a person who has passionately loved me, and is one of the most deserving women in the world; on the other side, I shall draw upon myself an implacable hatred that will ruin my fortune, and perhaps proceed somewhat further." "I do not comprehend what you say," replied the Duke de Nemours, "but I begin to see that the reports we have had of your interest in a great Princess are not wholly without ground." "They are not," replied the Viscount, "but I would to God they were: you would not see me in the perplexity I am in; but I must relate the whole affair to you, to convince you how much I have to fear.

"Ever since I came to Court, the Queen has treated me with a great deal of favour and distinction, and I had grounds to believe that she was very kindly disposed towards me: there was nothing, however, particular in all this, and I never presumed to entertain any thoughts of her but what were full of respect; so far from it, that I was deeply in love with Madam de Themines; anyone that sees her may easily judge, 'tis very possible for one to be greatly in love with her, when one is beloved by her, and so I was. About two years ago, the Court being at Fontainebleau, I was two or three times in conversation with the Queen, at hours when there were very few people in her apartment: it appeared to me, that my turn of wit was agreeable to her, and I observed she always approved what I said. One day among others she fell into a discourse concerning confidence. I said there was nobody in whom I entirely confided, that I found people always repented of having done so, and that I knew a great many things of which I had never spoke: the Queen told me, she esteemed me the more for it, that she had not found in France anyone that could keep a secret, and that this was what had embarrassed her more than anything else, because it had deprived her of the pleasure of having a confidant; that nothing was so necessary in life as to have somebody one could open one's mind to with safety, especially for people of her rank. Afterwards she frequently resumed the same discourse, and acquainted me with very particular circumstances; at last I imagined she was desirous to learn my secrets, and to entrust me with her own; this thought engaged me strictly to her. I was so pleased with this distinction that I made my court to her with greater assiduity than usual. One evening the King and the ladies of the Court rode out to take the air in the forest, but the Queen, being a little indisposed did not go; I stayed to wait upon her, and she walked down to the pond-side, and dismissed her gentlemen ushers, that she might be more at liberty. After she had taken a few turns she came up to me, and bid me follow her; 'I would speak with you,' says she, 'and by what I shall say you will see I am your friend.' She stopped here, and looking earnestly at me; 'You are in love,' continued she, 'and because perhaps you have made nobody your confidant, you think that your love is not known; but it is known, and even by persons who are interested in it: you are observed, the place where you see your mistress is discovered, and there's a design to surprise you; I don't know who she is, nor do I ask you to tell me, I would only secure you from the misfortunes into which you may fall.' See, I beseech you, what a snare the Queen laid for me, and how difficult it was for me not to fall into it; she had a mind to know if I was in love, and as she did not ask me who I was in love with, but let me see her intention was only to serve me, I had no suspicion that she spoke either out of curiosity or by design.

"Nevertheless, contrary to all probability, I saw into the bottom of the matter; I was in love with Madam de Themines, but though she loved me again, I was not happy enough to have private places to see her in without danger of being discovered there, and so I was satisfied she could not be the person the Queen meant; I knew also, that I had an intrigue with another woman less handsome and less reserved than Madam de Themines, and that it was not impossible but the place where I saw her might be discovered; but as this was a business I little cared for, it was easy for me to guard against all sorts of danger by forbearing to see her; I resolved therefore to acknowledge nothing of it to the Queen, but to assure her on the contrary that I had a long time laid aside the desire of gaining women's affections, even where I might hope for success, because I found them all in some measure unworthy of engaging the heart of an honourable man, and that it must be something very much above them which could touch me. 'You do not answer me ingenuously,' replied the Queen; 'I am satisfied of the contrary; the free manner in which I speak to you ought to oblige you to conceal nothing from me; I would have you,' continued she, 'be of the number of my friends; but I would not, after having admitted you into that rank, be ignorant of your engagements; consider, whether you think my friendship will be too dear at the price of making me your confidant; I give you two days to think on it; but then, consider well of the answer you shall make me, and remember that if ever I find hereafter you have deceived me, I shall never forgive you as long as I live.'

"Having said this, the Queen left me without waiting for my answer; you may imagine how full my thoughts were of what she had said to me; the two days she had given me to consider of it I did not think too long a time to come to a resolution; I found she had a mind to know if I was in love, and that her desire was I should not be so; I foresaw the consequences of what I was going to do, my vanity was flattered with the thought of having a particular interest with the Queen, and a Queen whose person is still extremely amiable; on the other hand, I was in love with Madam de Themines, and though I had committed a petty treason against her by my engagement with the other woman I told you of, I could not find in my heart to break with her; I foresaw also the danger I should expose myself to, if I deceived the Queen, and how hard it would be to do it; nevertheless I could not resolve to refuse what fortune offered me, and was willing to run the hazard of anything my ill conduct might draw upon me; I broke with her with whom I kept a correspondence that might be discovered, and was in hopes of concealing that I had with Madam de Themines.

"At the two days' end, as I entered the room where the Queen was with all the ladies about her, she said aloud to me, and with a grave air that was surprising enough, 'Have you thought of the business I charged you with, and do you know the truth of it?' 'Yes, Madam,' answered I, 'and 'tis as I told your Majesty.' 'Come in the evening, when I am writing,' replied she, 'and you shall have further orders.' I made a respectful bow without answering anything, and did not fail to attend at the hour she had appointed me. I found her in the gallery, with her secretary and one of her women. As soon as she saw me she came to me, and took me to the other end of the gallery; 'Well,' says she, 'after having considered thoroughly of this matter, have you nothing to say to me, and as to my manner of treating you, does not it deserve that you should deal sincerely with me?' 'It is, Madam,' answered I, 'because I deal sincerely, that I have nothing more to say, and I swear to your Majesty with all the respect I owe you, that I have no engagement with any woman of the Court.' 'I will believe it,' replied the Queen, 'because I wish it; and I wish it, because I desire to have you entirely mine, and because it would be impossible for me to be satisfied with your friendship, if you were in love; one cannot confide in those who are; one cannot be secure of their secrecy; they are too much divided, and their mistresses have always the first place in their thoughts, which does not suit at all with the manner in which I would have you live with me: remember then, it is upon your giving me your word that you have no engagement, that I choose you for my confidant; remember, I insist on having you entirely to myself, and that you shall have no friend of either sex but such as I shall approve, and that you abandon every care but that of pleasing me; I'll not desire you to neglect any opportunity for advancing your fortune; I'll conduct your interests with more application than you can yourself, and whatever I do for you, I shall think myself more than recompensed, if you answer my expectations; I make choice of you, to open my heart's griefs to you, and to have your assistance in softening them; you may imagine they are not small; I bear in appearance without much concern the King's engagement with the Duchess of Valentinois, but it is insupportable to me; she governs the King, she imposes upon him, she slights me, all my people are at her beck. The Queen, my daughter-in-law, proud of her beauty, and the authority of her uncles, pays me no respect. The Constable Montmorency is master of the King and kingdom; he hates me, and has given proofs of his hatred, which I shall never forget. The Mareschal de St. Andre is a bold young favourite, who uses me no better than the others. The detail of my misfortunes would move your pity; hitherto I have not dared to confide in anybody, I confide in you, take care that I never repent it, and be my only consolation.' The Queen blushed, when she had ended this discourse, and I was so truly touched with the goodness she had expressed to me, that I was going to throw myself at her feet: from that day she has placed an entire confidence in me, she has done nothing without advising with me, and the intimacy and union between us still subsists.

III

"In the meantime, however busy and full I was of my new engagement with the Queen, I still kept fair with Madam de Themines by a natural inclination which it was not in my power to conquer; I thought she cooled in her love to me, and whereas, had I been prudent, I should have made use of the change I observed in her for my cure, my love redoubled upon it, and I managed so ill that the Queen got some knowledge of this intrigue. Jealousy is natural to persons of her nation, and perhaps she had a greater affection for me than she even imagined herself; at least the report of my being in love gave her so much uneasiness, that I thought myself entirely ruined with her; however I came into favour again by virtue of submissions, false oaths, and assiduity; but I should not have been able to have deceived her long, had not Madam de Themines's change disengaged me from her against my will; she convinced me she no longer loved me, and I was so thoroughly satisfied of it, that I was obliged to give her no further uneasiness, but to let her be quiet. Some time after she wrote me this letter which I have lost; I learned from it, she had heard of the correspondence I had with the other woman I told you of, and that that was the reason of her change. As I had then nothing further left to divide me, the Queen was well enough satisfied with me; but the sentiments I have for her not being of a nature to render me incapable of other engagements, and love not being a thing that depends on our will, I fell in love with Madam de Martigues, of whom I was formerly a great admirer, while she was with Villemontais, maid of honour to the Queen-Dauphin; I have reason to believe she does not hate me; the discretion I observe towards her, and which she does not wholly know the reasons of, is very agreeable to her; the Queen has not the least suspicion on her account, but she has another jealousy which is not less troublesome; as Madam de Martigues is constantly with the Queen-Dauphin, I go there much oftener than usual; the Queen imagines that 'tis this Princess I am in love with; the Queen-Dauphin's rank, which is equal to her own, and the superiority of her youth and beauty, create a jealousy that rises even to fury, and fills her with a hatred against her daughter-in-law that cannot be concealed. The Cardinal of Loraine, who, I believe has been long aspiring to the Queen's favour, and would be glad to fill the place I possess, is, under pretence of reconciling the two Queens, become master of the differences between them; I doubt not but he has discovered the true cause of the Queen's anger, and I believe he does me all manner of ill offices, without letting her see that he designs it. This is the condition my affairs are in at present; judge what effect may be produced by the letter which I have lost, and which I unfortunately put in my pocket with design to restore it to Madam de Themines: if the Queen sees this letter, she will know I have deceived her; and that almost at the very same time that I deceived her for Madam de Themines, I deceived Madam de Themines for another; judge what an idea this will give her of me, and whether she will ever trust me again. If she does not see the letter, what shall I say to her? She knows it has been given to the Queen-Dauphin; she will think Chatelart knew that Queen's hand, and that the letter is from her; she will fancy the person of whom the letter expresses a jealousy, is perhaps herself; in short, there is nothing which she may not think, and there is nothing which I ought not to fear from her thoughts; add to this, that I am desperately in love with Madam de Martigues, and that the Queen-Dauphin will certainly show her this letter, which she will conclude to have been lately writ. Thus shall I be equally embroiled both with the person I love most, and with the person I have most cause to fear. Judge, after this, if I have not reason to conjure you to say the letter is yours, and to beg of you to get it out of the Queen-Dauphin's hands."

"I am very well satisfied," answered the Duke de Nemours, "that one cannot be in a greater embarrassment than that you are in, and it must be confessed you deserve it; I have been accused of being inconstant in my amours, and of having had several intrigues at the same time, but you out-go me so far, that I should not so much as have dared to imagine what you have undertaken; could you pretend to keep Madam de Themines, and be at the same engaged with the Queen? did you hope to have an engagement with the Queen, and be able to deceive her? she is both an Italian and a Queen, and by consequence full of jealousy, suspicion, and pride. As soon as your good fortune, rather than your good conduct, had set you at liberty from an engagement you was entangled in, you involved yourself in new ones, and you fancied that in the midst of the Court you could be in love with Madam de Martigues without the Queen's perceiving it: you could not have been too careful to take from her the shame of having made the first advances; she has a violent passion for you; you have more discretion than to tell it me, and I than to ask you to tell it; it is certain she is jealous of you, and has truth on her side." "And does it belong to you," interrupted the Viscount, "to load me with reprimands, and ought not your own experience to make you indulgent to my faults? However I grant I am to blame; but think, I conjure you, how to draw me out of this difficulty"; "I think you must go to the Queen-Dauphin as soon as she is awake, and ask her for the letter, as if you had lost it." "I have told you already," replied the Duke de Nemours, "that what you propose is somewhat extraordinary, and that there are difficulties in it which may affect my own particular interest; but besides, if this letter has been seen to drop out of your pocket, I should think it would be hard to persuade people that it dropped out of mine." "I thought I had told you," replied the Viscount, "that the Queen-Dauphin had been informed that you dropped it." "How," said the Duke de Nemours hastily, apprehending the ill consequence this mistake might be of to him with Madam de Cleves, "has the Queen-Dauphin been told I dropped the letter?" "Yes," replied the Viscount, "she has been told so; and what occasioned the mistake was, that there were several gentlemen of the two Queens in a room belonging to the tennis court, where our clothes were put up, when your servants and mine went together to fetch them; then it was the letter fell out of the pocket; those gentlemen took it up, and read it aloud; some believed it belonged to you, and others to me; Chatelart, who took it, and to whom I have just sent for it, says, he gave it to the Queen-Dauphin as a letter of yours; and those who have spoken of it to the Queen have unfortunately told her it was mine; so that you may easily do what I desire of you, and free me from this perplexity."

The Duke de Nemours had always had a great friendship for the Viscount de Chartres, and the relation he bore to Madam de Cleves still made him more dear to him; nevertheless he could not prevail with himself to run the risk of her having heard of this letter, as of a thing in which he was concerned; he fell into a deep musing, and the Viscount guessed pretty near what was the subject of his meditations; "I plainly see," said he, "that you are afraid of embroiling yourself with your mistress, and I should almost fancy the Queen-Dauphin was she, if the little jealousy you seem to have of Monsieur d'Anville did not take me off from that thought; but be that as it will, it is not reasonable you should sacrifice your repose to mine, and I'll put you in a way of convincing her you love, that this letter is directed to me, and not to you; here is a billet from Madam d'Amboise, who is a friend of Madam de Themines, and was her confidant in the amour between her and me; in this she desires me to send her Madam de Themines's letter, which I have lost; my name is on the superscription, and the contents of the billet prove, without question, that the letter she desires is the same with that which has been found; I'll leave this billet in your hands, and agree that you may show it to your mistress in your justification; I conjure you not to lose a moment, but to go this morning to the Queen-Dauphin."

The Duke de Nemours promised the Viscount he would, and took Madam d'Amboise's billet; nevertheless his design was not to see the Queen-Dauphin; he thought more pressing business required his care; he made no question, but she had already spoke of the letter to Madam de Cleves, and could not bear that a person he loved so desperately, should have ground to believe he had engagements with any other.

He went to the Princess of Cleves as soon as he thought she might be awake; and ordered her to be told, that, if he had not business of the last consequence, he would not have desired the honour to see her at so extraordinary an hour. Madam de Cleves was in bed, and her mind was tossed to and fro by a thousand melancholy thoughts that she had had during the night; she was extremely surprised to hear the Duke de Nemours asked for her; the anxiety she was in made her presently answer, that she was ill, and could not speak with him.

The Duke was not at all shocked at this refusal; he thought it presaged him no ill, that she expressed a little coldness at a time when she might be touched with jealousy. He went to the Prince of Cleves's apartment, and told him he came from that of his lady, and that he was very sorry he could not see her, because he had an affair to communicate to her of great consequence to the Viscount de Chartres; he explained in few words to the Prince the importance of this business, and the Prince immediately introduced him into his lady's chamber. Had she not been in the dark, she would have found it hard to have concealed the trouble and astonishment she was in to see the Duke de Nemours introduced by her husband. Monsieur de Cleves told her the business was about a letter, wherein her assistance was wanting for the interest of the Viscount, that she was to consult with Monsieur de Nemours what was to be done; and that as for him he was going to the King, who had just sent for him.

The Duke de Nemours had his heart's desire, in being alone with Madam de Cleves; "I am come to ask you, Madam," said he, "if the Queen-Dauphin has not spoke to you of a letter which Chatelart gave her yesterday." "She said something to me of it," replied Madam de Cleves, "but I don't see what relation this letter his to the interests of my uncle, and I can assure you that he is not named in it." "It is true, Madam," replied the Duke de Nemours, "he is not named in it but yet it is addressed to him, and it very much imports him that you should get it out of the Queen-Dauphin's hands." "I cannot comprehend," replied the Princess, "how it should be of any consequence to him, if this letter should be seen, nor what reason there is to redemand it in his name." "If you please to be at leisure to hear me, Madam," said Monsieur de Nemours, "I'll presently make you acquainted with the true state of the thing, and inform you of matters of so great importance to the Viscount, that I would not even have trusted the Prince of Cleves with them, had I not stood in need of his assistance to have the honour to see you." "I believe," said Madam de Cleves in a very unconcerned manner, "that anything you may give yourself the trouble of telling me, will be to little purpose; you had better go to the Queen-Dauphin, and plainly tell her, without using these roundabout ways, the interest you have in that letter, since she has been told, as well as I, that it belongs to you."

The uneasiness of mind which Monsieur de Nemours observed in Madam de Cleves gave him the most sensible pleasure he ever knew, and lessened his impatience to justify himself: "I don't know, Madam," replied he, "what the Queen-Dauphin may have been told; but I am not at all concerned in that letter; it is addressed to the Viscount." "I believe so," replied Madam de Cleves, "but the Queen-Dauphin has heard to the contrary, and she won't think it very probable that the Viscount's letters should fall out of your pocket; you must therefore have some reason, that I don't know of, for concealing the truth of this matter from the Queen-Dauphin; I advise you to confess it to her." "I have nothing to confess to her," says he, "the letter is not directed to me, and if there be anyone that I would have satisfied of it, it is not the Queen-Dauphin; but, Madam, since the Viscount's interest is nearly concerned in this, be pleased to let me acquaint you with some matters that are worthy of your curiosity." Madam de Cleves by her silence showed her readiness to hear him, and he as succinctly as possible related to her all he had just heard from the Viscount. Though the circumstances were naturally surprising, and proper to create attention, yet Madam de Cleves heard them with such coldness, that she seemed either not to believe them true, or to think them indifferent to her; she continued in this temper until the Duke de Nemours spoke of Madam d'Amboise's billet, which was directed to the Viscount, and was a proof of all he had been saying; as Madam de Cleves knew that this lady was a friend of Madam de Themines, she found some probability in what the Duke de Nemours had said, which made her think, that the letter perhaps was not addressed to him; this thought suddenly, and in spite of herself, drew her out of the coldness and indifferency she had until then been in. The Duke having read the billet, which fully justified him, presented it to her to read, and told her she might possibly know the hand. She could not forbear taking it, and examining the superscription to see if it was addressed to the Viscount de Chartres, and reading it all over, that she might the better judge, if the letter which was redemanded was the same with that she had in her hand. The Duke de Nemours added whatever he thought proper to persuade her of it; and as one is easily persuaded of the truth of what one wishes, he soon convinced Madam de Cleves that he had no concern in the letter.

She began now to reason with him concerning the embarrassment and danger the Viscount was in, to blame his ill conduct, and to think of means to help him: she was astonished at the Queen's proceedings, and confessed to the Duke that she had the letter; in short, she no sooner believed him innocent, but she discoursed with him with greater ease and freedom, concerning what she would scarce before vouchsafe to hear; they agreed that the letter should not be restored to the Queen-Dauphin, for fear she should show it to Madam de Martigues, who knew Madam de

Themines's hand, and would easily guess, by the interest she had in the Viscount, that it was addressed to him; they agreed also, that they ought not to entrust the Queen-Dauphin with all that concerned the Queen her mother-in-law. Madam de Cleves, under pretence of serving her uncle, was pleased to be the Duke de Nemours's confidant in the secrets he had imparted to her.

The Duke would not have confined his discourse to the Viscount's concerns, but from the liberty he had of free conversation with her, would have assumed a boldness he had never yet done, had not a message been brought in to Madam de Cleves, that the Queen-Dauphin had sent for her. The Duke was forced to withdraw; he went to the Viscount to inform him, that after he had left him, he thought it more proper to apply to Madam de Cleves, his niece, than to go directly to the Queen-Dauphin; he did not want reasons to make him approve what he had done, and to give him hopes of good success.

In the meantime Madam de Cleves dressed herself in all haste to go to the Queen-Dauphin; she was no sooner entered her chamber, but she called her to her, and whispered her, "I have been waiting for you these two hours, and was never so perplexed about disguising a truth as I have been this morning: the Queen has heard of the letter I gave you yesterday, and believes it was the Viscount de Chartres that dropped it; you know, she has some interest to be satisfied in it; she has been in search for the letter, and has caused Chatelart to be asked for it; who said he had given it to me; they have been to ask me for it, under pretence it was an ingenious letter which the Queen had a curiosity to see; I durst not say that you had it, for fear she should think I had given it you on your uncle the Viscount's account, and that there was a correspondence between him and me. I was already satisfied that his seeing me so often gave her uneasiness, so that I said the letter was in the clothes I had on yesterday, and that those who had them in keeping were gone abroad; give me the letter immediately," added she, "that I may send it her, and that I may read it before I send it to see if I know the hand."

Madam de Cleves was harder put to it than she expected; "I don't know, Madam, what you will do," answered she, "for Monsieur de Cleves, to whom I gave it to read, returned it to the Duke of Nemours, who came early this morning to beg him to get it of you. Monsieur de Cleves had the imprudence to tell him he had it, and the weakness to yield to the entreaties the Duke de Nemours made that he would restore it him." "You throw me into the greatest embarrassment I can possibly be in," replied the Queen-Dauphin; "and you have given this letter to the Duke de Nemours. Since it was I that gave it you, you ought not to have restored it without my leave; what would you have me say to the Queen, and what can she imagine? She will think, and not without reason, that this letter concerns myself, and that there is something between the Viscount and me; she will never be persuaded the letter belonged to the Duke de Nemours." "I am very much concerned," replied Madam de Cleves, "for the misfortune I have occasioned, and I believe the difficulty I have brought you into is very great; but 'twas Monsieur de Cleves's fault, and not mine." "You are in fault," replied the Queen-Dauphin, "for having given him the letter; and I believe you are the only woman in the world that acquaints her husband with all she knows." "I acknowledge myself in fault, Madam," replied the Princess of Cleves, "but let us rather think of preventing the consequences of what I have done, than insist on the fault itself." "Do you remember, pretty near, what the letter contains?" says the Queen-Dauphin. "Yes, Madam, I do," replied she, "for I have read it over more than once." "If so," said the Queen-Dauphin, "you must immediately get it written out in an unknown hand, and I'll send it to the Queen; she'll not show it those who have seen it already; and though she should, I'll stand in it, that it is the same Chatelart gave me; and he'll not dare to say otherwise."

Madam de Cleves approved of this expedient, and the more because it gave her an opportunity of sending for the Duke de Nemours, to have the letter itself again, in order to have it copied word for word, imitating as near as may be the hand it was written in, and she thought this would effectually deceive the Queen. As soon as she was got home, she informed her husband of what had passed between her and the Queen-Dauphin, and begged him to send for the Duke de Nemours. The Duke was sent for, and came immediately; Madam de Cleves told him all she had told her husband, and asked for the letter; but the Duke answered, that he had already returned it to the Viscount de Chartres, who was so overjoyed upon having it again, and being freed from the danger he was in, that he sent it immediately to Madam de Themines's friend. Madam de Cleves was in a new embarrassment on this occasion: in short, after having consulted together, they resolved to form the letter by memory; and, in order to go about it, they locked themselves up, and left orders that nobody should be admitted, and that all the Duke de Nemours's attendants should be sent away. Such an appearance of secret confidence was no small charm to Monsieur de Nemours, and even to Madam de Cleves; her husband's presence, and the interests of her uncle the Viscount de Chartres, were considerations which in great measure removed her scruples, and made this opportunity of seeing and being with the Duke de Nemours so agreeable to her, that she never before experienced a joy so pure and free from allay; this threw her into a freedom and gaiety of spirit which the Duke had never observed in her till now, and which made him still more passionately in love with her: as he had never known such agreeable moments, his vivacity was much heightened; and whenever Madam de Cleves was beginning to recollect and write the letter, instead of assisting her seriously, did nothing but interrupt her with wit and pleasantry. Madam de Cleves was as gay as he, so that they had been locked up a considerable time, and two messages had come from the Queen-Dauphin to hasten Madam de Cleves, before they had half finished the letter.

The Duke de Nemours was glad to prolong the time that was so agreeable to him, and neglected the concerns of his friend; Madam de Cleves was not at all tired, and neglected also the concerns of her uncle: at last, with much ado, about four o'clock the letter was finished, and was so ill done, and the copy so unlike the original, as to the handwriting, that the queen must have taken very little care to come at the truth of the matter, if she had been imposed on by so ill a counterfeit. Accordingly she was not deceived; and however industrious they were to persuade her, that this letter was addressed to the Duke de Nemours, she remained satisfied not only that it was addressed to the Viscount de Chartres, but that the Queen-Dauphin was concerned in it, and that there was a correspondence between them; this heightened her hatred against that Princess to such a degree, that she never forgave her, and never ceased persecuting her till she had driven her out of France.

As for the Viscount de Chartres, his credit was entirely ruined with her; and whether the Cardinal of Loraine had already insinuated himself so far into her esteem as to govern her, or whether the accident of this letter, which made it appear that the Viscount had deceived her, enabled her to discover the other tricks he had played her, it is certain he could never after entirely reconcile himself to her; their correspondence was broke off, and at length she ruined him by means of the conspiracy of Amboise, in which he was involved.

After the letter was sent to the Queen-Dauphin, Monsieur de Cleves and Monsieur de Nemours went away; Madam de Cleves continued alone, and being no longer supported by the joy which the presence of what one loves gives one, she seemed like one newly waked from a dream; she beheld, with astonishment, the difference between the condition she was in the night before, and that she was in at this time: she called to mind, how cold and sullen she was to the Duke de Nemours, while she thought Madam de Themines's letter was addressed to him, and how calm and sweet a situation of mind succeeded that uneasiness, as soon as he was satisfied he was not concerned in that letter; when she reflected, that she reproached herself as guilty for having given him the foregoing day only some marks of sensibility, which mere compassion might have produced, and that by her peevish humour this morning, she had expressed such a jealousy as was a certain proof of passion, she thought she was not herself; when she reflected further, that the Duke de Nemours saw plainly that she knew he was in love with her, and that, notwithstanding her knowing it, she did not use him the worse for it, even in her husband's presence; but that, on the contrary, she had never behaved so favourably to him; when she considered, she was the cause of Monsieur de Cleves's sending for him, and that she had just passed an afternoon in private with him; when she considered all this, she found, there was something within her that held intelligence with the Duke de Nemours, and that she deceived a husband who least deserved it; and she was ashamed to appear so little worthy of esteem, even in the eyes of her lover; but what she was able to support less than all the rest was, the remembrance of the condition in which she spent the last night, and the pricking griefs she felt from a suspicion that the Duke de Nemours was in love with another, and that she was deceived by him.

Never till then was she acquainted with the dreadful inquietudes that flow from jealousy and distrust; she had applied all her cares to prevent herself from falling in love with the Duke de Nemours, and had not before had any fear of his being in love with another: though the suspicions which this letter had given her were effaced, yet they left her sensible of the hazard there was of being deceived, and gave her impressions of distrust and jealousy which she had never felt till that time; she was surprised that she had never yet reflected how improbable it was that a man of the Duke de Nemours's turn, who had showed so much inconstancy towards women, should be capable of a lasting and sincere passion; she thought it next to impossible for her to be convinced of the truth of his love; "But though I could be convinced of it," says she, "what have I to do in it? Shall I permit it? Shall I make a return? Shall I engage in gallantry, be false to Monsieur de Cleves, and be false to myself? In a word, shall I go to expose myself to the cruel remorses and deadly griefs that rise from love? I am subdued and vanquished by a passion, which hurries me away in spite of myself; all my resolutions are vain; I had the same thoughts yesterday that I have today, and I act today contrary to what I resolved yesterday; I must convey myself out of the sight of the Duke de Nemours; I must go into the country, however fantastical my journey may appear; and if Monseur de Cleves is obstinately bent to hinder me, or to know my reasons for it, perhaps I shall do him and myself the injury to acquaint him with them." She continued in this resolution, and spent the whole evening at home, without going to the Queen-Dauphin to enquire what had happened with respect to the counterfeited letter.

When the Prince of Cleves returned home, she told him she was resolved to go into the country; that she was not very well, and had occasion to take the air. Monsieur de Cleves, to whom she appeared so beautiful that he could not think her indisposition very considerable, at first made a jest of her design, and answered that she had forgot that the nuptials of the Princesses and the tournament were very near, and that she had not too much time to prepare matters so as to appear there as magnificently as other ladies. What her husband said did not make her change her resolution, and she begged he would agree, that while he was at Compiegne with the King, she might go to Colomiers, a pretty house then building, within a day's journey of Paris. Monsieur de Cleves consented to it; she went thither with a design of not returning so soon, and the King set out for Compiegne, where he was to stay but few days.

The Duke de Nemours was mightily concerned he had not seen Madam de Cleves since that afternoon which he had spent so agreeably with her, and which had increased his hopes; he was so impatient to see her again that he could not rest; so that when the King returned to Paris, the Duke resolved to go to see his sister the Duchess de Mercoeur, who was at a country seat of hers very near Colomiers; he asked the Viscount to go with him, who readily consented to it. The Duke de Nemours did this in hopes of visiting Madam de Cleves, in company of the Viscount.

Madam de Mercoeur received them with a great deal of joy, and thought of nothing but giving them all the pleasures and diversions of the country; one day, as they were hunting a stag, the Duke de Nemours lost himself in the forest, and upon enquiring his way was told he was near Colomiers; at that word, Colomiers, without further reflection, or so much as knowing what design he was upon, he galloped on full speed the way that had been showed him; as he rode along he came by chance to the made-ways and walks, which he judged led to the castle: at the end of these walks he found a pavilion, at the lower end of which was a large room with two closets, the one opening into a flower-garden, and the other looking into a spacious walk in the park; he entered the pavilion, and would have stopped to observe the beauty of it, if he had not seen in the walk the Prince and Princess of Cleves, attended with a numerous train of their domestics. As he did not expect to meet Monsieur de Cleves there, whom he had left with the King, he thought at first of hiding himself; he entered the closet which looked into the flower-garden, with design to go out that way by a door which opened to the forest; but observing Madam de Cleves and her husband were sat down under the pavilion, and that their attendants stayed in the park, and could not come to him without passing by the place where Monsieur and Madam de Cleves were, he could not deny himself the pleasure of seeing this Princess, nor resist the curiosity he had to hear her conversation with a husband, who gave him more jealousy than any of his rivals. He heard Monsieur de Cleves say to his wife, "But why will you not return to Paris? What can keep you here in the country? You have of late taken a fancy for solitude, at which I am both surprised and concerned, because it deprives me of your company: I find too, you are more melancholy than usual, and I am afraid you have some cause of grief." "I have nothing to trouble my mind," answered she with an air of confusion, "but there is such a bustle at Court, and such a multitude of people always at your house, that it is impossible but both body and mind should be fatigued, and one cannot but desire repose." "Repose," answered he, "is not very proper for one of your age; you are at home, and at Court, in such a manner as cannot occasion weariness, and I am rather afraid you desire to live apart from me." "You would do me great wrong to think so," replied she with yet more confusion, "but I beg you to leave me here; if you could stay here, and without company, I should be very glad of it; nothing would be more agreeable to me than your conversation in this retirement, provided you would approve not to have about you that infinite number of people, who in a manner never leave you." "Ah! Madam," cries Monsieur de Cleves, "both your looks and words convince me that you have reasons to desire to be alone, which I don't know; I conjure you to tell them me." He urged her a great while to inform him, without being able to oblige her to it; and after she had excused herself in a manner which still increased her husband's curiosity, she continued in a deep silence, with her eyes cast down then, taking up the discourse on a sudden, and looking upon him, "Force me not," said she, "to confess a thing to you which I have not the power to confess, though I have often designed it; remember only, that it is not prudent a woman of my years, and mistress of her own conduct, should remain exposed in the midst of a Court." "What is it, Madam," cried Monsieur de Cleves, "that you lead me to imagine? I dare not speak it, for fear of offending you." Madam de Cleves making no answer, her silence confirmed her husband in what he thought; "You say nothing to me," says he, "and that tells me clearly, that I am not mistaken." "Alas, sir," answered she, falling on her knees, "I am going to make a confession to you, such as no woman ever yet made to her husband; but the innocence of my intentions, and of my conduct, give me power to do it; it is true, I have reasons to absent myself from Court, and I would avoid the dangers persons of my age are sometimes liable to; I have never shown any mark of weakness, and I cannot apprehend I ever shall, if you will permit me to retire from Court, since now I have not Madam de Chartres to assist me in my conduct; however dangerous a step I am taking, I take it with pleasure to preserve myself worthy of you; I ask you a thousand pardons, if I have sentiments which displease you, at least I will never displease you by my actions; consider, that to do what I do, requires more friendship and esteem for a husband than ever wife had; direct my conduct, have pity on me, and if you can still love me."

Monsieur de Cleves, all the while she spoke, continued leaning his head on his hand, almost beside himself, and never thought of raising her up. When she had done speaking, and he cast his eyes upon her, and saw her on her knees with her face drowned in tears, inimitably beautiful, he was ready to die for grief, and taking her up in his arms, "Have you pity on me, Madam," says he, "for I deserve it, and pardon me, if in the first moments of an affliction so violent as mine, I do not answer as I ought to so generous a proceeding as yours; I think you more worthy of esteem and admiration than any woman that ever was, but I find myself also the most unfortunate of men: you inspired me with passion the first moment I saw you, and that passion has never decayed; not your coldness, nor even enjoyment itself, has been able to extinguish it; it still continues in its first force, and yet it has not been in my power to kindle in your breast any spark of love for me, and now I find you fear you have an inclination for another; and who is he, Madam, this happy man that gives you such apprehensions? How long has he charmed you? What has he done to charm you? What method has he taken to get into your heart? When I could not gain your affections myself, it was some comfort to me to think, that no other could gain them; in the meantime, another has effected what I could not, and I have at once the jealousy of a husband and lover. But it is impossible for me to retain that of a husband after such a proceeding on your part, which is too noble and ingenuous not to give me an entire security; it even comforts me as a lover; the sincerity you have expressed, and the confidence you have placed in me are of infinite value: you have esteem enough for me to believe I shall not abuse the confession you have made to me; you are in the right, Madam, I will not abuse it, or love you the less for it; you make me unhappy by the greatest mark of fidelity ever woman gave her husband; but go on, Madam, and inform me who he is whom you would avoid." "I beg you not to ask me," replied she; "I am resolved not to tell you, nor do I think it prudent to name him." "Fear not, Madam," replied Monsieur de Cleves, "I know the world too well to be ignorant that a woman's having a husband does not hinder people from being in love with her; such lovers may be the objects of one's hatred, but we are not to complain of it; once again, Madam, I conjure you to tell me what I so much desire to know." "It is in vain to press me," replied she, "I have the power to be silent in what I think I ought not to tell; the confession I made to you was not owing to any weakness, and it required more courage to declare such a truth than it would have done to conceal it."

The Duke de Nemours did not lose a word of this conversation, and what Madam de Cleves had said gave him no less jealousy than her husband; he was so desperately in love with her, that he believed all the world was so too; it is true, he had many rivals, yet he fancied them still more, and his thoughts wandered to find out who it was Madam de Cleves meant: he had often thought he was not disagreeable to her, but the grounds of his judgment on this occasion appeared so slight, that he could not imagine he had raised in her heart a passion violent enough to oblige her to have recourse to so extraordinary a remedy; he was so transported, that he scarce knew what he saw, and he could not pardon Monsieur de Cleves for not having pressed his wife enough to tell him the name of the person she concealed from him.

Monsieur de Cleves nevertheless used his utmost endeavours to know it; and having urged her very much on the subject; "I think," answered she, "that you ought to be satisfied with my sincerity; ask me no more about it, and don't give me cause to repent of what I have done; content yourself with the assurance which I once more give you, that my sentiments have never appeared by any of my actions, and that no address hath been made to me that could give me offence." "Ah! Madam," replied Monsieur de Cleves on a sudden, "I cannot believe it; I remember the confusion you was in when your picture was lost; you have given away, Madam, you have given away that picture, which was so dear to me, and which I had so just a right to; you have not been able to conceal your inclinations, you are in love; it is known; your virtue has hitherto saved you from the rest." "Is it possible," cried Madam de Cleves, "you can imagine there was any reserve or disguise in a confession like mine, which I was no way obliged to? Take my word, I purchase dearly the confidence I desire of you; I conjure you to believe I have not given away my picture; it is true, I saw it taken, but I would not seem to see it, for fear of subjecting myself to hear such things as no one has yet dared to mention to me." "How do you know then that you are loved," said Monsieur de Cleves? "What mark, what proof of it has been given you?" "Spare me the pain," replied she, "of repeating to you circumstances which I am ashamed to have observed, and which have convinced me but too much of my own weakness." "You are in the right, Madam," answered he, "I am unjust; always refuse me when I ask you such things, and yet don't be angry with me for asking them."

Just then several of the servants, who had stayed in the walks, came to acquaint Monsieur de Cleves, that a gentleman was arrived from the King, with orders for him to be at Paris that evening. Monsieur de Cleves was obliged to go, and had only time to tell his wife that he desired her to come to Paris the next day; and that he conjured her to believe, that however afflicted he was, he had a tenderness and esteem for her, with which she ought to be satisfied.

When he was gone, and Madam de Cleves being alone, considered what she had done, she was so frightened at the thought of it, she could hardly believe it to be true. She found she had deprived herself of the heart and esteem of her husband, and was involved in a labyrinth she should never get out of; she asked herself why she had ventured on so dangerous a step, and perceived she was engaged in it almost without having designed it; the singularity of such a confession, for which she saw no precedent, made her fully sensible of her danger.

But on the other hand, when she came to think that this remedy, however violent it was, was the only effectual one she could make use of against Monsieur de Nemours, she found she had no cause to repent, or to believe she had ventured too far; she passed the whole night full of doubts, anxiety and fear; but at last her spirits grew calm again; she even felt a pleasure arise in her mind, from a sense of having given such a proof of fidelity to a husband who deserved it so well, who had so great a friendship and esteem for her, and had so lately manifested it by the manner in which he received the confession she had made him.

In the meantime Monsieur de Nemours was gone away from the place, in which he had overheard a conversation which so sensibly affected him, and was got deep into the forest; what Madam de Cleves said of her picture had revived him, since it was certain from thence that he was the person she had an inclination for; at first he gave a leap of joy, but his raptures were at an end as soon as he began to reflect, that the same thing that convinced him he had touched the heart of Madam de Cleves, ought to convince him also that he should never receive any marks of it, and that it would be impossible to engage a lady who had recourse to so extraordinary a remedy; and yet he could not but be sensibly pleased to have reduced her to that extremity; he thought it glorious for him to have gained the affections of a woman so different from the rest of her sex; in a word, he thought himself very happy and very unhappy at the same time. He was benighted in the forest, and was very much put to it to find his way again to his sister's the Duchess of Mercoeur; he arrived there at break of day, and was extremely at a loss what account to give of his absence, but he made out the matter as well as he could, and returned that very day to Paris with the Viscount.

The Duke was so taken up with his passion, and so surprised at the conversation he had heard, that he fell into an indiscretion very common, which is, to speak one's own particular sentiments in general terms, and to relate one's proper adventures under borrowed names. As they were travelling he began to talk of love, and exaggerated the pleasure of being in love with a person that deserved it; he spoke of the fantastical effects of this passion, and at last not being able to contain within himself the admiration he was in at the action of Madam de Cleves, he related it to the Viscount without naming the person, or owning he had any share in it; but he told it with so much warmth and surprise, that the Viscount easily suspected the story concerned himself. The Viscount urged him very much to confess it, and told him he had known a great while that he was violently in love, and that it was unjust in him to show a distrust of a man who had committed to him a secret on which his life depended. The Duke de Nemours was too much in love to own it, and had always concealed it from the Viscount, though he valued him the most of any man at Court; he answered that one of his friends had told him this adventure, and made him promise not to speak of it; and he also conjured the Viscount to keep the secret: the Viscount assured him he would say nothing of it but notwithstanding Monsieur de Nemours repented that he had told him so much.

In the meantime Monsieur de Cleves was gone to the King, with a heart full of sorrow and affliction. Never had husband so violent a passion for his wife, or so great an esteem; what she had told him did not take away his esteem of her, but made it of a different nature from that he had had before; what chiefly employed his thoughts, was a desire to guess who it was that had found out the secret to win her heart; the Duke de Nemours was the first person he thought of on this occasion, as being the handsomest man at Court; and the Chevalier de Guise, and the Mareschal de St. Andre occurred next, as two persons who had made it their endeavour to get her love, and who were still very assiduous in courting her, so that he was fully persuaded it must be one of the three. He arrived at the Louvre, and the King carried him into his closet to inform him he had made choice of him to conduct Madame into Spain, and that he believed nobody could acquit himself better of that charge, nor that any lady would do France greater honour than Madam de Cleves. Monsieur de Cleves received the honour the King had done him by this choice with the respect he ought, and he considered it also as what would take his wife from Court, without leaving room to suspect any change in her conduct; but the embarrassment he was under required a speedier remedy than that journey, which was to be deferred a great while, could afford; he immediately wrote to Madam de Cleves to acquaint her with what the King had told him, and gave her to understand he absolutely expected she should return to Paris. She returned according to his orders, and when they met, they found one another overwhelmed with melancholy.

Monsieur de Cleves spoke to her, as a man of the greatest honour in the world, and the best deserving the confidence she had reposed in him; "I am not alarmed as to your conduct," said he, "you have more strength and virtue than you imagine; I am not alarmed with fears of what may happen hereafter; what troubles me is that I see you have those sentiments for another which you want for me." "I don't know what to answer you," said she, "I die with shame when I speak of this subject spare me, I conjure you, such cruel conversations; regulate my conduct, and never let me see anybody; this is all I desire of you; but take it not ill of me, if I speak no more of a thing which makes me appear so little worthy of you, and which I think so unbecoming me." "You are in the right, Madam;" replied he, "I abuse your goodness and your confidence in me; but have some compassion also on the condition you have brought me to, and think that whatever you have told me, you conceal from me a name, which creates in me a curiosity I cannot live without satisfying; and yet I ask you not to satisfy it; I cannot, however, forbear telling you, that I believe the man I am to envy is the Mareschal de St. Andre, the Duke de Nemours, or the Chevalier de Guise." "I shall make you no answer," says she blushing, "nor give you any ground from what I say, either to lessen or strengthen your suspicions; but if you endeavour to inform yourself by observing me, you will throw me into a confusion all the world will take notice of, for God's sake," continued she, "allow me under pretence of an indisposition to see nobody." "No, Madam," said he, "it will quickly be discovered to be a feigned business; and besides, I am unwilling to trust you to anything but yourself; my heart tells me this is the best way I can take, and my reason tells me so also, considering the temper of mind you are in, I cannot put a greater restraint upon you than by leaving you to your liberty."

Monsieur de Cleves was not mistaken; the confidence he showed he had in his wife, fortified her the more against Monsieur de Nemours, and made her take more severe resolutions than any restraint could have brought her to. She went to wait on the Queen-Dauphin at the Louvre as she used to do, but avoided the presence and eyes of Monsieur de Nemours with so much care, that she deprived him of almost all the joy he had in thinking she loved him; he saw nothing in her actions but what seemed to show the contrary; he scarcely knew if what he had heard was not a dream, so very improbable it seemed to him; the only thing which assured him that he was not mistaken, was Madam de Cleves's extreme melancholy, which appeared, whatever pains she took to hide it; and perhaps kind words and looks would not have increased the Duke of Nemours's love so much as this severe conduct did.

One evening, as Monsieur and Madam de Cleves were at the Queen's apartment, it was said there was a report that the King would name another great lord to wait on Madame into Spain. Monsieur de Cleves had his eye fixed on his wife, when it was further said, the Chevalier de Guise, or the Mareschal de St. Andre, was the person; he observed she was not at all moved at either of those names, nor the discourse of their going along with her; this made him believe, it was not either of them whose presence she feared. In order to clear up his suspicions, he went into the Queen's closet, where the King then was, and after having stayed there some time came back to his wife, and whispered her, that he had just heard the Duke de Nemours was the person designed to go along with them to Spain.

The name of the Duke de Nemours, and the thought of being exposed to see him every day, during a very long journey, in her husband's presence, so affected Madam de Cleves, that she could not conceal her trouble: and being willing to give other reasons for it, "No choice," says she, "could have been made more disagreeable for you; he will share all honours with you, and I think you ought to endeavour to get some other chosen." "It is not honour, Madam," replied Monsieur de Cleves, "that makes you apprehensive of the Duke de Nemours's going with me, the uneasiness you are in proceeds from another cause; and from this uneasiness of yours I learn, that which I should have discovered in another woman, by the joy she would have expressed on such an occasion; but be not afraid; what I have told you is not true, it was an invention of mine to assure myself of a thing which I already believed but too much."

Having said this, he went out, being unwilling to increase, by his presence, the concern he saw his wife in.

The Duke de Nemours came in that instant, and presently observed Madam de Cleves's condition; he came up to her, and told her softly, he had that respect for her, he durst not ask what it was made her more pensive than usual. The voice of the Duke de Nemours brought her to herself again, and looking at him, without having heard what he had said to her, full of her own thoughts, and afraid lest her husband should see him with her, "For God's sake," says she, "leave me to myself in quiet." "Alas, Madam," answered he, "I disturb you too little; what is it you can complain of? I dare not speak to you, I dare not look upon you, I tremble whenever I approach you. How have I drawn upon myself what you have said to me, and why do you show me that I am in part the cause of the trouble I see you in?" Madam de Cleves was very sorry to have given the Duke an opportunity of explaining himself more clearly than ever he had done before; she left him without making any answer, and went home with her mind more agitated than ever. Her husband perceived her concern was increased, and that she was afraid he would speak to her of what had passed, and followed her into her closet; "Do not shun me, Madam," says he, "I will say nothing to you that shall displease you; I ask pardon for the surprise I gave you a while ago; I am sufficiently punished by what I have learnt from it; the Duke de Nemours was of all men he whom I most feared; I see the danger you are in; command yourself for your own sake, and, if it is possible, for mine; I do not ask this of you as a husband, but as a man whose happiness wholly depends on you, and who loves you more violently and more tenderly than he whom your heart prefers to me." Monsieur de Cleves was melted upon speaking these words, and could scarce make an end of them; his wife was so moved, she burst into tears, and embraced him with a tenderness and sorrow that put him into a condition not very different from her own; they continued silent a while, and parted without having the power to speak to one another.

All things were ready for the marriage of Madame, and the Duke of Alva was arrived to espouse her; he was received with all the ceremony and magnificence that could be displayed on such an occasion; the King sent to meet him the Prince of Conde, the Cardinals of Loraine and Guise, the Dukes of Loraine and Ferrara, d'Aumale, de Bouillon, de Guise, and de Nemours; they had a great number of gentlemen, and a great many pages in livery; the King himself, attended with two hundred gentlemen, and the Constable at their head, received the Duke of Alva at the first gate of the Louvre; the Duke would have kneeled down, but the King refused it, and made him walk by his side to the Queen's apartment, and to Madame's, to whom the Duke of Alva had brought a magnificent present from his master; he went thence to the apartment of Madam Margaret the King's sister, to compliment her on the part of the Duke of Savoy, and to assure her he would arrive in a few days; there were great assemblies at the Louvre, the show the Duke of Alva, and the Prince of Orange who accompanied him, the beauties of the Court.

Madam de Cleves could not dispense with going to these assemblies, however desirous she was to be absent, for fear of disobliging her husband, who absolutely commanded her to be there; and what yet more induced her to it, was the absence of the Duke de Nemours; he was gone to meet the Duke of Savoy, and after the arrival of that Prince, he was obliged to be almost always with him, to assist him in everything relating to the ceremonies of the nuptials; for this reason Madam de Cleves did not meet him so often as she used to do, which gave her some sort of ease.

The Viscount de Chartres had not forgot the conversation he had had with the Duke de Nemours: it still ran in his mind that the adventure the Duke had related to him was his own; and he observed him so carefully that it is probable he would have unravelled the business, if the arrival of the Duke of Alva and of the Duke of Savoy had not made such an alteration in the Court, and filled it with so much business, as left no opportunities for a discovery of that nature; the desire he had to get some information about it, or rather the natural disposition one has to relate all one knows to those one loves, made him acquaint Madam de Martigues with the extraordinary action of that person who had confessed to her husband the passion she had for another; he assured her the Duke de Nemours was the man who had inspired so violent a love, and begged her assistance in observing him. Madam de Martigues was glad to hear what the Viscount told her, and the curiosity she had always observed in the Queen-Dauphin for what concerned the Duke de Nemours made her yet more desirous to search into the bottom of the affair.

A few days before that which was fixed for the ceremony of the marriage, the Queen-Dauphin entertained at supper the King her father-in-law, and the Duchess of Valentinois. Madam de Cleves, who had been busy in dressing herself, went to the Louvre later than ordinary; as she was going, she met a gentleman that was coming from the Queen-Dauphin to fetch her; as soon as she entered the room, that Princess, who was sitting upon her bed, told her aloud, that she had expected her with great impatience. "I believe, Madam," answered she, "that I am not obliged to you for it, and that your impatience was caused by something else, and not your desire to see me." "You are in the right," answered the Queen-Dauphin, "but, nevertheless, you are obliged to me; for I'll tell you an adventure, which I am sure you'll be glad to know."

Madam de Cleves kneeled at her bedside, and, very luckily for her, with her face from the light: "You know," said the Queen, "how desirous we have been to find out what had caused so great a change in the Duke de Nemours; I believe I know it, and it is what will surprise you; he is desperately in love with, and as much beloved by, one of the finest ladies of the Court." It is easy to imagine the grief Madam de Cleves felt upon hearing these words, which she could not apply to herself, since she thought nobody knew anything of her passion for the Duke; "I see nothing extraordinary in that," replied she, "considering how young and handsome a man the Duke de Nemours is." "No," replied the Queen-Dauphin, "there is nothing extraordinary in it; but what will surprise you is, that this lady, who is in love with the Duke de Nemours, has never given him any mark of it, and that the fear she was in lest she should not always be mistress of her passion, has made her confess it to her husband, that he may take her away from Court; and it is the Duke de Nemours himself who has related what I tell you."

If Madam de Cleves was grieved at first through the thought that she had no concern in this adventure, the Queen-Dauphin's last words threw her into an agony, by making it certain she had too much in it; she could not answer, but continued leaning her head on the bed; meanwhile the Queen went on, and was so intent on what she was saying, that she took no notice of her embarrassment. When Madam de Cleves was a little come to herself, "This story, Madam," says she, "does not seem very probable to me, and I should be glad to know who told it you." "It was Madam de Martigues," replied the Queen-Dauphin, "and she heard it from the Viscount de Chartres; you know the Viscount is in love with her; he entrusted this matter to her as a secret, and he was told it by the Duke de Nemours himself; it is true the Duke did not tell the lady's name, nor acknowledge that he was the person she was in love with, but the Viscount makes no manner of question of it." When the Queen-Dauphin had done speaking, somebody came up to the bed; Madam de Cleves was so placed that she could not see who it was, but she was presently convinced, when the Queen-Dauphin cried out with an air of gaiety and surprise, "Here he is himself, I'll ask him what there is in it." Madam de Cleves knew very well it was the Duke de Nemours, without turning herself, as it really was; upon which she went up hastily to the Queen-Dauphin, and told her softly, that she ought to be cautious of speaking to him of this adventure, which he had entrusted to the Viscount de Chartres as a secret, and that it was a thing which might create a quarrel between them. "You are too wise," said the Queen-Dauphin smiling, and turned to the Duke de Nemours. He was dressed for the evening assembly, and taking up the discourse with that grace which was natural to him, "I believe, Madam," says he, "I may venture to think you were speaking of me as I came in, that you had a design to ask me something, and that Madam de Cleves is against it." "It is true," replied the Queen-Dauphin, "but I shall not be so complaisant to her on this occasion as I was used to be; I would know of you, whether a story I have been told is true, and whether you are not the person who is in love with, and beloved by a lady of the Court, who endeavours to conceal her passion from you, and has confessed it to her husband."

The concern and confusion Madam de Cleves was in was above all that can be imagined, and if death itself could have drawn her out of this condition, she would have gladly embraced it; but the Duke de Nemours was yet more embarrassed if possible: the discourse of the Queen-Dauphin, by whom he had reason to believe he was not hated, in the presence of Madam de Cleves, who was confided in by her more than anybody of the Court, and who confided more in her, threw him into such confusion and extravagance of thought, that it was impossible for him to be master of his countenance: the concern he saw Madam de Cleves in through his fault, and the thought of having given her just cause to hate him, so shocked him he could not speak a word. The Queen-Dauphin, seeing how thunderstruck she was, "Look upon him, look upon him," said she to Madam de Cleves, "and judge if this adventure be not his own."

In the meantime the Duke de Nemours, finding of what importance it was to him to extricate himself out of so dangerous a difficulty, recovered himself from his first surprise, and became at once master of his wit and looks. "I acknowledge, Madam," said he, "it is impossible to be more surprised and concerned than I was at the treachery of the Viscount de Chartres, in relating an adventure of a friend of mine, which I had in confidence imparted to him. I know how to be revenged of him," continued he, smiling with a calm air, which removed the suspicions the Queen-Dauphin had entertained of him: "He has entrusted me with things of no very small importance; but I don't know, Madam, why you do me the honour to make me a party in this affair. The Viscount can't say I am concerned in it, for I told him the contrary; I may very well be taken to be a man in love, but I cannot believe, Madam, you will think me of the number of those who are loved again." The Duke was glad to say anything to the Queen-Dauphin, which alluded to the inclination he had expressed for her formerly, in order to divert her thoughts from the subject in question. She imagined she understood well enough the drift of what he said, but without making any answer to it, she continued to rally him upon the embarrassment he was in. "I was concerned, Madam," said he, "for the interest of my friend, and on account of the just reproaches he might make me for having told a secret which is dearer to him than life. He has nevertheless entrusted me but with one half of it, and has not told me the name of the person he loves; all I know is, that he's the most deeply in love of any man in the world, and has the most reason to complain." "Do you think he has reason to complain," replied the Queen-Dauphin, "when he is loved again?" "Do you believe he is, Madam," replied he, "and that a person who had a real passion could discover it to her husband? That lady, doubtless, is not acquainted with love, and has mistaken for it a slight acknowledgment of the fondness her lover had for her. My friend can't flatter himself with the lent hopes; but, unfortunate as he is, he thinks himself happy at least in having made her afraid of falling in love with him, and he would not change his condition for that of the happiest lover in the world." "Your friend has a passion very easy to be satisfied," said the Queen-Dauphin, "and I begin to believe it is not yourself you are speaking of; I am almost," continued she, "of the opinion of Madam de Cleves, who maintains that this story cannot be true." "I don't really believe it can be true," answered Madam de Cleves, who had been silent hitherto; "and though it were possible to be true, how should it have been known? It is very unlikely that a woman, capable of so extraordinary a resolution, would have the weakness to publish it; and surely her husband would not have told it neither, or he must be a husband very unworthy to have been dealt with in so generous a manner." The Duke de Nemours, who perceived the suspicions Madam de Cleves had of her husband, was glad to confirm her in them, knowing he was the most formidable rival he had to overcome. "Jealousy," said he, "and a curiosity perhaps of knowing more than a wife has thought fit to discover, may make a husband do a great many imprudent things."

Madam de Cleves was put to the last proof of her power and courage, and not being able to endure the conversation any longer, she was going to say she was not well, when by good fortune for her the Duchess of Valentinois came in, and told the Queen-Dauphin that the King was just coming; the Queen-Dauphin went into the closet to dress herself, and the Duke de Nemours came up to Madam de Cleves as she was following her.

"I would give my life, Madam," said he, "to have a moment's conversation with you; but though I have a world of important things to say to you, I think nothing is more so, than to entreat you to believe, that if I have said anything in which the Queen-Dauphin may seem concerned, I did it for reasons which do not relate to her." Madam de Cleves pretended not to hear him, and left him without giving him a look, and went towards the King, who was just come in. As there were abundance of people there, she trod upon her gown, and made a false step, which served her as an excuse to go out of a place she had not the power to stay in, and so pretending to have received some hurt she went home.

Monsieur de Cleves came to the Louvre, and was surprised not to find his wife there; they told him of the accident that had befallen her, and he went immediately home to enquire after her; he found her in bed, and perceived her hurt was not considerable. When he had been some time with her, he found her so excessive melancholy that he was surprised at it; "What ails you, Madam?" says he; "you seem to have some other grief than that which you complain of." "I feel the most sensible grief I can ever experience," answered she; "what use have you made of that extraordinary, or rather foolish confidence which I placed in you? Did not I deserve to have my secret kept? and though I had not deserved it, did not your own interest engage you to it? Should your curiosity to know a name it was not reasonable for me to tell you have obliged you to make a confidant to assist you in the discovery? Nothing but that curiosity could have made you guilty of so cruel an indiscretion; the consequences of it are as bad as they possibly can be. This adventure is known, and I have been told it by those who are not aware that I am principally concerned in it." "What do you say, Madam?" answered he; "you accuse me of having told what passed between you and me, and you inform me that the thing is known; I don't go about to clear myself from this charge, you can't think me guilty of it; without doubt you have applied to yourself what was told you of some other." "Ah! Sir," replied she, "the world has not an adventure like mine, there is not another woman capable of such a thing. The story I have heard could not have been invented by chance; nobody could imagine any like it; an action of this nature never entered any thoughts but mine. The Queen-Dauphin has just told me the story; she had it from the Viscount de Chartres, and the Viscount from the Duke de Nemours." "The Duke de Nemours!" cried Monsieur de Cleves, like a man transported and desperate: "How! does the Duke de Nemours know that you are in love with him, and that I am acquainted with it?" "You are always for singling out the Duke de Nemours rather than any other," replied she; "I have told you I will never answer you concerning your suspicions: I am ignorant whether the Duke de Nemours knows the part I have in this adventure, and that which you have ascribed to him; but he told it to the Viscount de Chartres, and said he had it from one of his friends, who did not name the lady: this friend of the Duke de Nemours must needs be one of yours, whom you entrusted the secret to, in order to clear up your suspicions." "Can one have a friend in the world, in whom one would repose such a confidence," replied Monsieur de Cleves, "and would a man clear his suspicions at the price of informing another with what one would wish to conceal from oneself? Think rather, Madam, to whom you have spoken; it is more probable this secret should have escaped from you than from me; you was not able alone to support the trouble you found yourself in, and you endeavoured to comfort yourself by complaining to some confidant who has betrayed you."

"Do not wholly destroy me," cried she, "and be not so hard-hearted as to accuse me of a fault you have committed yourself: can you suspect me of it? and do you think, because I was capable of informing you of this matter, I was therefore capable of informing another?"

The confession which Madam de Cleves had made to her husband was so great a mark of her sincerity, and she so strongly denied that she had entrusted it to any other, that Monsieur de Cleves did not know what to think. On the other hand he was sure he had never said anything of it; it was a thing that could not have been guessed, and yet it was known; it must therefore come from one of them two; but what grieved him most was to know that this secret was in the hands of somebody else, and that in all probability it would be soon divulged.

Madam de Cleves thought much after the same manner; she found it equally impossible that her husband should, or should not have spoken of it. What the Duke de Nemours had said to her, that curiosity might make a husband do indiscreet things, seemed so justly applicable to Monsieur de Cleves's condition, that she could not think he said it by chance, and the probability of this made her conclude that Monsieur de Cleves had abused the confidence she had placed in him. They were so taken up, the one and the other, with their respective thoughts, that they continued silent a great while; and when they broke from this silence, they only repeated the same things they had already said very often; their hearts and affections grew more and more estranged from each other.

It is easy to imagine how they passed the night; Monsieur de Cleves could no longer sustain the misfortune of seeing a woman whom he adored in love with another; he grew quite heartless, and thought he had reason to be so in an affair where his honour and reputation were so deeply wounded: he knew not what to think of his wife, and was at a loss what conduct he should prescribe to her, or what he should follow himself; he saw nothing on all sides but precipices and rocks; at last, after having been long tossed to and fro in suspense, he considered he was soon to set out for Spain, and resolved to do nothing which might increase the suspicion or knowledge of his unfortunate condition. He went to his wife, and told her that what they had to do was not to debate between themselves who had discovered the secret; but to make it appear that the story which was got abroad was a business in which she had no concern; that it depended upon her to convince the Duke de Nemours and others of it; that she had nothing to do but to behave herself to him with that coldness and reserve which she ought to have for a man who professed love to her; that by this proceeding she would easily remove the opinion he entertained of her being in love with him; and therefore she needed not to trouble herself as to what he might hitherto have thought, since if for the future she discovered no weakness, his former thoughts would vanish of themselves; and that especially she ought to frequent the Louvre and the assemblies as usual.

Having said this, Monsieur de Cleves left his wife without waiting her answer; she thought what he said very reasonable, and the resentment she had against the Duke de Nemours made her believe she should be able to comply with it with a great deal of ease; but it seemed a hard task to her to appear at the marriage with that freedom and tranquillity of spirit as the occasion required. Nevertheless as she was to carry the Queen-Dauphin's train, and had been distinguished with that honour in preference to a great many other Princesses, it was impossible to excuse herself from it without making a great deal of noise and putting people upon enquiring into the reasons of it. She resolved therefore to do her utmost, and employed the rest of the day in preparing herself for it, and in endeavouring to forget the thoughts that gave her so much uneasiness; and to this purpose she locked herself up in her closet. Of all her griefs the most violent was that she had reason to complain of the Duke de Nemours, and could find no excuse to urge in his favour; she could not doubt but he had related this adventure to the Viscount de Chartres; he had owned it himself, nor could she any more doubt from his manner of speaking of it, but that he knew the adventure related to her; how could she excuse so great an imprudence? and what was become of that extreme discretion which she had so much admired in this Prince? "He was discreet," said she, "while he was unhappy; but the thought of being happy, though on uncertain grounds, has put an end to his discretion; he could not consider that he was beloved, without desiring to have it known; he said everything he could say; I never acknowledged it was he I was in love with; he suspected it, and has declared his suspicions; if he had been sure of it, he might have acted as he has; I was to blame for thinking him a man capable of concealing what flattered his vanity; and yet it is for this man, whom I thought so different from other men, that I am become like other women, who was so unlike them before. I have lost the heart and esteem of a husband who ought to have been my happiness; I shall soon be looked upon by all the world as a person led away by an idle and violent passion; he for whom I entertain this passion is no longer ignorant of it; and it was to avoid these misfortunes that I hazarded my quiet, and even my life." These sad reflections were followed by a torrent of tears; but however great her grief was, she plainly perceived she should be able to support it, were she but satisfied in the Duke de Nemours.

The Duke was no less uneasy than she; the indiscretion he had been guilty of in telling what he did to the Viscount de Chartres, and the mischievous consequences of it, vexed him to the heart; he could not represent to himself the affliction and sorrow he had seen Madam de Cleves in without being pierced with anguish; he was inconsolable for having said things to her about this adventure, which, though gallant enough in themselves, seemed on this occasion too gross and impolite, since they gave Madam de Cleves to understand he was not ignorant that she was the woman who had that violent passion, and that he was the object of it. It was before the utmost of his wishes to have a conversation with her, but now he found he ought rather to fear than desire it. "What should I say to her!" says he; "should I go to discover further to her what I have made her too sensible of already! Shall I tell how I know she loves me; I, who have never dared to say I loved her? Shall I begin with speaking openly of my passion, that she may see my hopes have inspired me with boldness? Can I even think of approaching her, and of giving her the trouble to endure my sight? Which way could I justify myself? I have no excuse, I am unworthy of the least regard from Madam de Cleves, and I even despair of her ever looking upon me: I have given her by my own fault better means of defending herself against me than any she was searching for, and perhaps searching for to no purpose. I lose by my imprudence the glory and happiness of being loved by the most beautiful and deserving lady in the world; but if I had lost this happiness, without involving her in the most extreme grief and sufferings at the same time, I should have had some comfort; for at this moment I am more sensible of the harm I have done her, than of that I have done myself in forfeiting her favour."

The Duke de Nemours continued turning the same thoughts over and over, and tormenting himself a great while; the desire he had to speak to Madam de Cleves came constantly into his mind; he thought of the means to do it; he thought of writing to her; but at last he found, considering the fault he had committed and the temper she was in, his best way was to show her a profound respect by his affliction and his silence, to let her see he durst not present himself before her, and to wait for what time, chance, and the inclination she had for him might produce to his advantage. He resolved also not to reproach the Viscount de Chartres for his unfaithfulness, for fear of confirming his suspicions.

The preparations for the espousals and marriage of Madame on the next day so entirely took up the thoughts of the Court, that Madam de Cleves and the Duke de Nemours easily concealed from the public their grief and uneasiness. The Queen-Dauphin spoke but slightly to Madam de Cleves of the conversation they had had with the Duke de Nemours; and Monsieur de Cleves industriously shunned speaking to his wife of what was past; so that she did not find herself under so much embarrassment as she had imagined.

The espousals were solemnised at the Louvre; and after the feast and ball all the Royal family went to lie at the Bishop's Palace, according to custom. In the morning, the Duke of Alva, who always had appeared very plainly dressed, put on a habit of cloth of gold, mixed with flame-colour, yellow and black, all covered over with jewels, and wore a close crown on his head. The Prince of Orange very richly dressed also, with his liveries, and all the Spaniards with theirs, came to attend the Duke of Alva from the Hotel de Villeroy where he lodged, and set out, marching four by four, till they came to the Bishop's Palace. As soon as he was arrived, they went in order to the Church; the King led Madame, who wore also a close crown, her train being borne by Mademoiselles de Montpensier and Longueville; the Queen came next, but without a crown; after her followed the Queen-Dauphin, Madame the King's sister, the Duchess of Loraine, and the Queen of Navarre, their trains being home by the Princesses; the Queens and the Princesses were all of them attended with their maids of honour, who were richly dressed in the same colour which they wore themselves; so that it was known by the colour of their habits whose maids they were: they mounted the place that was prepared in the Church, and there the marriage ceremonies were performed; they returned afterwards to dine at the Bishop's Palace, and went from thence about five o'clock to the Palace where the feast was, and where the Parliament, the Sovereign Courts, and the Corporation of the City were desired to assist. The King, the Queens, the Princes and Princesses sat at the marble table in the great hall of the Palace; the Duke of Alva sat near the new Queen of Spain, below the steps of the marble table, and at the King's right hand was a table for the ambassadors, the archbishops, and the Knights of the Order, and on the other side one for the Parliament.

The Duke of Guise, dressed in a robe of cloth of gold frieze, served the King as Great Chamberlain; the Prince of Conde as Steward of the Household, and the Duke de Nemours as Cup-bearer. After the tables were removed the ball began, and was interrupted by interludes and a great deal of extraordinary machinery; then the ball was resumed, and after midnight the King and the whole Court returned to the Louvre. However full of grief Madam de Cleves was, she appeared in the eyes of all beholders, and particularly in those of the Duke de Nemours, incomparably beautiful. He durst not speak to her, though the hurry of the ceremony gave him frequent opportunities; but he expressed so much sorrow and so respectful a fear of approaching her, that she no longer thought him to blame, though he had said nothing in his justification; his conduct was the same the following days, and wrought the same effect on the heart of Madam de Cleves.

At last the day of the tournament came; the Queens were placed in the galleries that were prepared for them; the four champions appeared at the end of the lists with a number of horses and liveries, the most magnificent sight that ever was seen in France.

The King's colours were white and black, which he always wore in honour of the Duchess of Valentinois, who was a widow. The Duke of Ferrara and his retinue had yellow and red. Monsieur de Guise's carnation and white. It was not known at first for what reason he wore those colours, but it was soon remembered that they were the colours of a beautiful young lady whom he had been in love with, while she was a maid, and whom he yet loved though he durst not show it. The Duke de Nemours had yellow and black; why he had them could not be found out: Madam de Cleves only knew the reason of it; she remembered to have said before him she loved yellow, and that she was sorry her complexion did not suit that colour. As for the Duke, he thought he might take that colour without any indiscretion, since not being worn by Madam de Cleves it could not be suspected to be hers.

The four champions showed the greatest address that can be imagined; though the King was the best horseman in his kingdom, it was hard to say which of them most excelled. The Duke de Nemours had a grace in all his actions which might have inclined to his favour persons less interested than Madam de Cleves. She no sooner saw him appear at the end of the lists, but her heart felt uncommon emotions, and every course he made she could scarce hide her joy when he had successfully finished his career.

In the evening, when all was almost over, and the company ready to break up, so it was for the misfortune of the State, that the King would needs break another lance; he sent orders to the Count de Montgomery, who was a very dextrous combatant, to appear in the lists. The Count begged the King to excuse him, and alleged all the reasons for it he could think of; but the King, almost angry, sent him word he absolutely commanded him to do it. The Queen conjured the King not to run any more, told him he had performed so well that he ought to be satisfied, and desired him to go with her to her apartments; he made answer, it was for her sake that he would run again; and entered the barrier; she sent the Duke of Savoy to him to entreat him a second time to return, but to no purpose; he ran; the lances were broke, and a splinter of the Count de Montgomery's lance hit the King's eye, and stuck there. The King fell; his gentlemen and Monsieur de Montmorency, who was one of the Mareschals of the field, ran to him; they were astonished to see him wounded, but the King was not at all disheartened; he said, that it was but a slight hurt, and that he forgave the Count de Montgomery. One may imagine what sorrow and affliction so fatal an accident occasioned on a day set apart to mirth and joy. The King was carried to bed, and the surgeons having examined his wound found it very considerable. The Constable immediately called to mind the prediction which had been told the King, that he should be killed in single fight; and he made no doubt but the prediction would be now accomplished. The King of Spain, who was then at Brussels, being advertised of this accident, sent his physician, who was a man of great reputation, but that physician judged the King past hope.

A Court so divided, and filled with so many opposite interests, could not but be in great agitation on the breaking out of so grand an event; nevertheless all things were kept quiet, and nothing was seen but a general anxiety for the King's health. The Queens, the Princes and Princesses hardly ever went out of his anti-chamber.

Madam de Cleves, knowing that she was obliged to be there, that she should see there the Duke de Nemours, and that she could not conceal from her husband the disorder she should be in upon seeing him, and being sensible also that the mere presence of that Prince would justify him in her eyes and destroy all her resolutions, thought proper to feign herself ill. The Court was too busy to give attention to her conduct, or to enquire whether her illness was real or counterfeit; her husband alone was able to come at the truth of the matter, but she was not at all averse to his knowing it. Thus she continued at home, altogether heedless of the great change that was soon expected, and full of her own thoughts, which she was at full liberty to give herself up to. Everyone went to Court to enquire after the King's health, and Monsieur de Cleves came home at certain times to give her an account of it; he behaved himself to her in the same manner he used to do, except when they were alone, and then there appeared something of coldness and reserve: he had not spoke to her again concerning what had passed, nor had she power, nor did she think it convenient to resume the discourse of it.

The Duke de Nemours, who had waited for an opportunity of speaking to Madam de Cleves, was surprised and afflicted not to have had so much as the pleasure to see her. The King's illness increased so much, that the seventh day he was given over by the physicians; he received the news of the certainty of his death with an uncommon firmness of mind; which was the more to be admired, considering that he lost his life by so unfortunate an accident, that he died in the flower of his age, happy, adored by his people, and beloved by a mistress he was desperately in love with. The evening before his death he caused Madame his sister to be married to the Duke of Savoy without ceremony. One may judge what condition the Duchess of Valentinois was in; the Queen would not permit her to see the King, but sent to demand of her the King's signets, and the jewels of the crown which she had in her custody. The Duchess enquired if the King was dead, and being answered, "No"; "I have then as yet no other matter," said she, "and nobody can oblige me to restore what he has trusted in my hands." As soon as the King expired at Chateau de Toumelles, the Duke of Ferrara, the Duke of Guise, and the Duke de Nemours conducted the Queen-Mother, the New King and the Queen-Consort to the Louvre. The Duke de Nemours led the Queen-Mother. As they began to march, she stepped back a little, and told the Queen her daughter-in-law, it was her place to go first; but it was easy to see, that there was more of spleen than decorum in this compliment.

IV

The Queen-mother was now wholly governed by the Cardinal of Loraine; the Viscount de Chartres had no interest with her, and the passion he had for Madam de Martigues and for liberty hindered him from feeling this loss as it deserved to be felt. The Cardinal, during the ten days' illness of the King, was at leisure to form his designs, and lead the Queen into resolutions agreeable to what he had projected; so that the King was no sooner dead but the Queen ordered the Constable to stay at Tournelles with the corpse of the deceased King in order to perform the usual ceremonies. This commission kept him at a distance and out of the scene of action; for this reason the Constable dispatched a courier to the King of Navarre, to hasten him to Court that they might join their interest to oppose the great rise of the House of Guise. The command of the Army was given to the Duke of Guise and the care of the finances to the Cardinal of Loraine. The Duchess of Valentinois was driven from Court; the Cardinal de Tournon, the Constable's declared enemy, and the Chancellor Olivier, the declared enemy of the Duchess of Valentinois, were both recalled. In a word, the complexion of the Court was entirely changed; the Duke of Guise took the same rank as the Princes of the blood, in carrying the King's mantle at the funeral ceremonies: He and his brothers carried all before them at Court, not only by reason of the Cardinal's power with the Queen-Mother, but because she thought it in her power to remove them should they give her umbrage; whereas she could not so easily remove the Constable, who was supported by the Princes of the blood.

When the ceremonial of the mourning was over, the Constable came to the Louvre, and was very coldly received by the King; he desired to speak with him in private, but the King called for Messieurs de Guise, and told him before them, that he advised him to live at ease; that the finances and the command of the Army were disposed of, and that when he had occasion for his advice, he would send for him to Court. The Queen received him in a yet colder manner than the King, and she even reproached him for having told the late King, that his children by her did not resemble him. The King of Navarre arrived, and was no better received; the Prince of Conde, more impatient than his brother, complained aloud, but to no purpose: he was removed from Court, under pretence of being sent to Flanders to sign the ratification of the peace. They showed the King of Navarre a forged letter from the King of Spain, which charged him with a design of seizing that King's fortresses; they put him in fear for his dominions, and made him take a resolution to go to Bearn; the Queen furnished him with an opportunity, by appointing him to conduct Madam Elizabeth, and obliged him to set out before her, so that there remained nobody at Court that could balance the power of the House of Guise.

Though it was a mortifying circumstance for Monsieur de Cleves not to conduct Madam Elizabeth, yet he could not complain of it, by reason of the greatness of the person preferred before him; he regretted the loss of this employment not so much on account of the honour he should have received from it, as because it would have given him an opportunity of removing his wife from Court without the appearance of design in it.

A few days after the King's death, it was resolved the new King should go to Rheims to be crowned. As soon as this journey was talked of, Madam de Cleves, who had stayed at home all this while under pretence of illness, entreated her husband to dispense with her following the Court, and to give her leave to go to take the air at Colomiers for her health: he answered, that whether her health was the reason or not of her desire, however he consented to it: nor was it very difficult for him to consent to a thing he had resolved upon before: as good an opinion as he had of his wife's virtue, he thought it imprudent to expose her any longer to the sight of a man she was in love with.

The Duke de Nemours was soon informed that Madam de Cleves was not to go along with the Court; he could not find in his heart to set out without seeing her, and therefore the night before his journey he went to her house as late as decency would allow him, in order to find her alone. Fortune favoured his intention; and Madam de Nevers and Madam de Martigues, whom he met in the Court as they were coming out, informed him they had left her alone. He went up in a concern and ferment of mind to be paralleled only by that which Madam de Cleves was under, when she was told the Duke de Nemours was come to see her; the fear lest he should speak to her of his passion, and lest she should answer him too favourably, the uneasiness this visit might give her husband, the difficulty of giving him an account of it, or of concealing it from him, all these things presented themselves to her imagination at once, and threw her into so great an embarrassment, that she resolved to avoid the thing of the world which perhaps she wished for the most. She sent one of her women to the Duke de Nemours, who was in her anti-chamber, to tell him that she had lately been very ill, and that she was sorry she could not receive the honour which he designed her. What an affliction was it to the Duke, not to see Madam de Cleves, and therefore not to see her, because she had no mind he should! He was to go away the next morning, and had nothing further to hope from fortune. He had said nothing to her since that conversation at the Queen-Dauphin's apartments, and he had reason to believe that his imprudence in telling the Viscount his adventure had destroyed all his expectations; in a word, he went away with everything that could exasperate his grief.

No sooner was Madam de Cleves recovered from the confusion which the thought of receiving a visit from the Duke had given her, but all the reasons which had made her refuse it vanished; she was even satisfied she had been to blame; and had she dared, or had it not been too late, she would have had him called back.

Madam de Nevers and Madam de Martigues went from the Princess of Cleves to the Queen-Dauphin's, where they found Monsieur de Cleves: the Queen-Dauphin asked them from whence they came; they said they came from Madam de Cleves, where they had spent part of the afternoon with a great deal of company, and that they had left nobody there but the Duke de Nemours. These words, which they thought so indifferent, were not such with Monsieur de Cleves: though he might well imagine the Duke de Nemours had frequent opportunities of speaking to his wife, yet the thought that he was now with her, that he was there alone, and that he might speak to her of his life, appeared to him at this time a thing so new and insupportable, that jealousy kindled in his heart with greater violence than ever. It was impossible for him to stay at the Queen's; he returned from thence, without knowing why he returned, or if he designed to go and interrupt the Duke de Nemours: he was no sooner come home, but he looked about him to see if there was anything by which he could judge if the Duke was still there; it was some comfort to him to find he was gone, and it was a pleasure to reflect that he could not have been long there: he fancied, that, perhaps, it was not the Duke de Nemours of whom he had reason to be jealous; and though he did not doubt of it, yet he endeavoured to doubt of it; but he was convinced of it by so many circumstances, that he continued not long in that pleasing uncertainty. He immediately went into his wife's room, and after having talked to her for some time about indifferent matters, he could not forbear asking her what she had done, and who she had seen, and accordingly she gave him an account: when he found she did not name the Duke de Nemours he asked her trembling, if those were all she had seen, in order to give her an occasion to name the Duke, and that he might not have the grief to see she made use of any evasion. As she had not seen him, she did not name him; when Monsieur de Cleves with accents of sorrow, said, "And have you not seen the Duke de Nemours, or have you forgot him?" "I have not seen him indeed," answered she; "I was ill, and I sent one of my women to make my excuses." "You was ill then only for him," replied Monsieur de Cleves, "since you admitted the visits of others: why this distinction with respect to the Duke de Nemours? Why is not he to you as another man? Why should you be afraid of seeing him? Why do you let him perceive that you are so? Why do you show him that you make use of the power which his passion gives you over him? Would you dare refuse to see him, but that you knew he distinguishes your rigour from incivility? But why should you exercise that rigour towards him? From a person like you, all things are favours, except indifference." "I did not think," replied Madam de Cleves, "whatever suspicions you have of the Duke de Nemours, that you could reproach me for not admitting a visit from him." "But I do reproach you, Madam," replied he, "and I have good ground for so doing; why should you not see him, if he has said nothing to you? but Madam, he has spoke to you; if his passion had been expressed only by silence, it would not have made so great an impression upon you; you have not thought fit to tell me the whole truth; you have concealed the greatest part from me; you have repented even of the little you have acknowledged, and you have not the resolution to go on; I am more unhappy than I imagined, more unhappy than any other man in the world: you are my wife, I love you as my mistress, and I see you at the same time in love with another, with the most amiable man of the Court, and he sees you every day, and knows you are in love with him: Alas! I believed that you would conquer your passion for him, but sure I had lost my reason when I believed it was possible." "I don't know," replied Madam de Cleves very sorrowfully, "whether you was to blame in judging favourably of so extraordinary a proceeding as mine; nor do I know if I was not mistaken when I thought you would do me justice." "Doubt it not, Madam," replied Monsieur de Cleves, "you was mistaken; you expected from me things as impossible as those I expected from you: how could you hope I should continue master of my reason? Had you forgot that I was desperately in love with you, and that I was your husband? Either of these two circumstances is enough to hurry a man into extremities; what may they not do both together? Alas! What do they not do? My thoughts are violent and uncertain, and I am not able to control them; I no longer think myself worthy of you, nor do I think you are worthy of me; I adore you, I hate you, I offend you, I ask your pardon, I admire you, I blush for my admiration: in a word, I have nothing of tranquillity or reason left about me: I wonder how I have been able to live since you spoke to me at Colomiers, and since you learned, from what the Queen-Dauphin told you, that your adventure was known; I can't discover how it came to be known, nor what passed between the Duke de Nemours and you upon the subject; you will never explain it to me, nor do I desire you to do it; I only desire you to remember that you have made me the most unfortunate, the most wretched of men."

Having spoke these words, Monsieur de Cleves left his wife, and set out the next day without seeing her; but he wrote her a letter full of sorrow, and at the same time very kind and obliging: she gave an answer to it so moving and so full of assurances both as to her past and future conduct, that as those assurances were grounded in truth, and were the real effect of her sentiments, the letter made great impressions on Monsieur de Cleves, and gave him some tranquillity; add to this that the Duke de Nemours going to the King as well as himself, he had the satisfaction to know that he would not be in the same place with Madam de Cleves. Everytime that lady spoke to her husband, the passion he expressed for her, the handsomeness of his behaviour, the friendship she had for him, and the thought of what she owed him, made impressions in her heart that weakened the idea of the Duke de Nemours; but it did not continue long, that idea soon returned more lively than before.

For a few days after the Duke was gone, she was hardly sensible of his absence; afterwards it tortured her; ever since she had been in love with him, there did not pass a day, but she either feared or wished to meet him, and it was a wounding thought to her to consider that it was no more in the power of fortune to contrive their meeting.

She went to Colomiers, and ordered to be carried thither the large pictures she had caused to be copied from the originals which the Duchess of Valentinois had procured to be drawn for her fine house of Annett. All the remarkable actions that had passed in the late King's reign were represented in these pieces, and among the rest was the Siege of Mets, and all those who had distinguished themselves at that Siege were painted much to the life. The Duke de Nemours was of this number, and it was that perhaps which had made Madam de Cleves desirous of having the pictures.

Madam de Martigues not being able to go along with the Court, promised her to come and pass some days at Colomiers. Though they divided the Queen's favour, they lived together without envy or coldness; they were friends, but not confidants; Madam de Cleves knew that Madam de Martigues was in love with the Viscount, but Madam de Martigues did not know that Madam de Cleves was in love with the Duke de Nemours, nor that she was beloved by him. The relation Madam de Cleves had to the Viscount made her more dear to Madam de Martigues, and Madam de Cleves was also fond of her as a person who was in love as well as herself, and with an intimate friend of her own lover.

Madam de Martigues came to Colomiers according to her promise, and found Madam de Cleves living in a very solitary manner: that Princess affected a perfect solitude, and passed the evenings in her garden without being accompanied even by her domestics; she frequently came into the pavilion where the Duke de Nemours had overheard her conversation with her husband; she delighted to be in the bower that was open to the garden, while her women and attendants waited in the other bower under the pavilion, and never came to her but when she called them. Madam de

Martigues having never seen Colomiers was surprised at the extraordinary beauty of it, and particularly with the pleasantness of the pavilion. Madam de Cleves and she usually passed the evenings there. The liberty of being alone in the night in so agreeable a place would not permit the conversation to end soon between two young ladies, whose hearts were enflamed with violent passions, and they took great pleasure in conversing together, though they were not confidants.

Madam de Martigues would have left Colomiers with great reluctance had she not quitted it to go to a place where the Viscount was; she set out for Chambort, the Court being there.

The King had been anointed at Rheims by the Cardinal of Loraine, and the design was to pass the rest of the summer at the castle of Chambort, which was newly built; the Queen expressed a great deal of joy upon seeing Madam de Martigues again at Court, and after having given her several proofs of it, she asked her how Madam de Cleves did, and in what manner she passed her time in the country. The Duke de Nemours and the Prince of Cleves were with the Queen at that time. Madam de Martigues, who had been charmed with Colomiers, related all the beauties of it, and enlarged extremely on the description of the pavilion in the forest, and on the pleasure Madam de Cleves took in walking there alone part of the night. The Duke de Nemours, who knew the place well enough to understand what Madam de Martigues said of it, thought it was not impossible to see Madam de Cleves there, without being seen by anybody but her. He asked Madam de Martigues some questions to get further lights; and the Prince of Cleves, who had eyed him very strictly while Madam de Martigues was speaking, thought he knew what his design was. The questions the Duke asked still more confirmed him in that thought, so that he made no doubt but his intention was to go and see his wife; he was not mistaken in his suspicions: this design entered so deeply into the Duke de Nemours's mind, that after having spent the night in considering the proper methods to execute it, he went betimes the next morning to ask the King's leave to go to Paris, on some pretended occasion.

Monsieur de Cleves was in no doubt concerning the occasion of his journey; and he resolved to inform himself as to his wife's conduct, and to continue no longer in so cruel an uncertainty; he had a desire to set out the same time as the Duke de Nemours did, and to hide himself where he might discover the success of the journey; but fearing his departure might appear extraordinary, and lest the Duke, being advertised of it, might take other measures, he resolved to trust this business to a gentleman of his, whose fidelity and wit he was assured of; he related to him the embarrassment he was under, and what the virtue of his wife had been till that time, and ordered him to follow the Duke de Nemours, to watch him narrowly, to see if he did not go to Colomiers, and if he did not enter the garden in the night.

The gentleman, who was very capable of this commission, acquitted himself of it with all the exactness imaginable. He followed the Duke to a village within half a league of Colomiers, where the Duke stopped and the gentleman easily guessed his meaning was to stay there till night. He did not think it convenient to wait there, but passed on, and placed himself in that part of the forest where he thought the Duke would pass: he took his measures very right; for it was no sooner night but he heard somebody coming that way, and though it was dark, he easily knew the Duke de Nemours; he saw him walk round the garden, as with a design to listen if he could hear anybody, and to choose the most convenient place to enter: the palisades were very high and double, in order to prevent people from coming in, so that it was very difficult for the Duke to get over, however he made a shift to do it. He was no sooner in the garden but he discovered where Madam de Cleves was; he saw a great light in the bower, all the windows of it were open; upon this, slipping along by the side of the palisades, he came up close to it, and one may easily judge what were the emotions of his heart at that instant: he took his station behind one of the windows, which served him conveniently to see what Madam de Cleves was doing. He saw she was alone; he saw her so inimitably beautiful, that he could scarce govern the transports which that sight gave him: the weather was hot, her head and neck were uncovered, and her hair hung carelessly about her. She lay on a couch with a table before her, on which were several baskets full of ribbons, out of which she chose some, and he observed she chose those colours which he wore at the tournament; he saw her make them up into knots for an Indian cane, which had been his, and which he had given to his sister; Madam de Cleves took it from her, without seeming to know it had belonged to the Duke. After she had finished her work with the sweetest grace imaginable, the sentiments of her heart showing themselves in her countenance, she took a wax candle and came to a great table over against the picture of the Siege of Mets, in which was the portrait of the Duke de Nemours; she sat down and set herself to look upon that portrait, with an attention and thoughtfulness which love only can give.

It is impossible to express what Monsieur de Nemours felt at this moment; to see, at midnight, in the finest place in the world, a lady he adored, to see her without her knowing that he saw her, and to find her wholly taken up with things that related to him, and to the passion which she concealed from him; this is what was never tasted nor imagined by any other lover.

The Duke was so transported and beside himself, that he continued motionless, with his eyes fixed on Madam de Cleves, without thinking how precious his time was; when he was a little recovered, he thought it best not to speak to her till she came into the garden, and he imagined he might do it there with more safety, because she would be at a greater distance from her women; but finding she stayed in the bower, he resolved to go in: when he was upon the point of doing it, what was his confusion; how fearful was he of displeasing her, and of changing that countenance, where so much sweetness dwelt, into looks of anger and resentment!

To come to see Madam de Cleves without being seen by her had no impudence in it, but to think of showing himself appeared very unwise; a thousand things now came into his mind which he had not thought of before; it carried in it somewhat extremely bold and extravagant, to surprise in the middle of the night a person to whom he had never yet spoke of his passion. He thought he had no reason to expect she would hear him, but that she would justly resent the danger to which he exposed her, by accidents which might rise from this attempt; all his courage left him, and he was several times upon the point of resolving to go back again without showing himself; yet urged by the desire of speaking to her, and heartened by the hopes which everything he had seen gave him, he advanced some steps, but in such disorder, that a scarf he had on entangled in the window, and made a noise. Madam de Cleves turned about, and whether her fancy was full of him, or that she stood in a place so directly to the light that she might know him, she thought it was he, and without the least hesitation or turning towards the place where he was, she entered the bower where her women were. On her entering she was in such disorder, that to conceal it she was forced to say she was ill; she said it too in order to employ her people about her, and to give the Duke time to retire. When she had made some reflection, she thought she had been deceived, and that her fancying she saw Monsieur de Nemours was only the effect of imagination. She knew he was at Chambort; she saw no probability of his engaging in so hazardous an enterprise; she had a desire several times to re-enter the bower, and to see if there was anybody in the garden. She wished perhaps as much as she feared to find the Duke de Nemours there; but at last reason and prudence prevailed over her other thoughts, and she found it better to continue in the doubt she was in, than to run the hazard of satisfying herself about it; she was a long time ere she could resolve to leave a place to which she thought the Duke was so near, and it was almost daybreak when she returned to the castle.

The Duke de Nemours stayed in the garden, as long as there was any light; he was not without hopes of seeing Madam de Cleves again, though he was convinced that she knew him, and that she went away only to avoid him; but when he found the doors were shut, he knew he had nothing more to hope; he went to take horse near the place where Monsieur de Cleves's gentleman was watching him; this gentleman followed him to the same village, where he had left him in the evening. The Duke resolved to stay there all the day, in order to return at night to Colomiers, to see if Madam de Cleves would yet have the cruelty to shun him or not expose herself to view: though he was very much pleased to find himself so much in her thoughts, yet was he extremely grieved at the same time to see her so naturally bent to avoid him.

Never was passion so tender and so violent as that of Monsieur de Nemours; he walked under the willows, along a little brook which ran behind the house, where he lay concealed; he kept himself as much out of the way as possible, that he might not be seen by anybody; he abandoned himself to the transports of his love, and his heart was so full of tenderness, that he was forced to let fall some tears, but those tears were such as grief alone could not shed; they had a mixture of sweetness and pleasure in them which is to be found only in love.

He set himself to recall to mind all the actions of Madam de Cleves ever since he had been in love with her; her cruelty and rigour, and that modesty and decency of behaviour she had always observed towards him, though she loved him; "For, after all, she loves me," said he, "she loves me, I cannot doubt of it, the deepest engagements and the greatest favours are not more certain proofs than those I have had. In the meantime, I am treated with the same rigour as if I were hated; I hoped something from time, but I have no reason to expect it any longer; I see her always equally on her guard against me and against herself; if I were not loved, I should make it my business to please; but I do please; she loves me, and tries to hide it from me. What have I then to hope, and what change am I to expect in my fortune? though I am loved by the most amiable person in the world, I am under that excess of passion which proceeds from the first certainty of being loved by her, only to make me more sensible of being ill used; let me see that you love me, fair Princess," cried he, "make me acquainted with your sentiments; provided I know them once in my life from you, I am content that you resume for ever the cruelties with which you oppress me; look upon me at least with the same eyes with which I saw you look that night upon my picture; could you behold that with such sweet complacency, and yet avoid me with so much cruelty? What are you afraid of? Why does my love appear so terrible to you? You love me, and you endeavour in vain to conceal it; you have even given me involuntary proofs of it; I know my happiness, permit me to enjoy it, and cease to make me unhappy. Is it possible I should be loved by the Princess of Cleves, and yet be unhappy? how beautiful was she last night? how could I forbear throwing myself at her feet? If I had done it, I might perhaps have hindered her from shunning me, my respectful behaviour would have removed her fears; but perhaps, after all, she did not know it was I; I afflict myself more than I need; she was only frightened to see a man at so unseasonable an hour."

These thoughts employed the Duke de Nemours all the day; he wished impatiently for the night, and as soon as it came he returned to Colomiers. Monsieur de Cleves's gentleman, who was disguised that he might be less observed, followed him to the place to which he had followed him the evening before, and saw him enter the garden again. The Duke soon perceived that Madam de Cleves had not run the risk of his making another effort to see her, the doors being all shut; he looked about on all sides to see if he could discover any light, but he saw none.

Madam de Cleves, suspecting he might return, continued in her chamber; she had reason to apprehend she should not always have the power to avoid him, and she would not submit herself to the hazard of speaking to him in a manner that would have been unsuitable to the conduct she had hitherto observed.

Monsieur de Nemours, though he had no hopes of seeing her, could not find in his heart soon to leave a place where she so often was; he passed the whole night in the garden, and found some pleasure at least in seeing the same objects which she saw every day; it was near sunrise before he thought of retiring; but as last the fear of being discovered obliged him to go away.

It was impossible for him to return to Court without seeing Madam de Cleves; he made a visit to his sister the Duchess of Mercoeur, at her house near Colomiers. She was extremely surprised at her brother's arrival; but he invented so probable a pretence for his journey, and conducted his plot so skilfully, that he drew her to make the first proposal herself of visiting Madam de Cleves. This proposal was executed that very day, and Monsieur de Nemours told his sister, that he would leave her at Colomiers, in order to go directly to the King; he formed this pretence of leaving her at Colomiers in hopes she would take her leave before him, and he thought he had found out by that means an infallible way of speaking to Madam de Cleves.

The Princess of Cleves, when they arrived, was walking in her garden the sight of Monsieur de Nemours gave her no small uneasiness, and put her out of doubt that it was he she had seen the foregoing night. The certainty of his having done so bold and imprudent a thing gave her some little resentment against him, and the Duke observed an air of coldness in her face, which sensibly grieved him; the conversation turned upon indifferent matters, and yet he had the skill all the while to show so much wit, complaisance, and admiration for Madam de Cleves, that part of the coldness she expressed towards him at first left her in spite of herself.

When his fears were over and he began to take heart, he showed an extreme curiosity to see the pavilion in the forest; he spoke of it as of the most agreeable place in the world, and gave so exact a description of it, that Madam de Mercoeur said he must needs have been there several times to know all the particular beauties of it so well. "And yet, I don't believe," replied Madam de Cleves, "that the Duke de Nemours was ever there; it has been finished but a little while." "It is not long since I was there," replied the Duke, looking upon her, "and I don't know if I ought not to be glad you have forgot you saw me there." Madam de Mercoeur, being taken up in observing the beauties of the gardens, did not attend to what her brother said; Madam de Cleves blushed, and with her eyes cast down, without looking on Monsieur de Nemours, "I don't remember," said she, "to have seen you there; and if you have been there, it was without my knowledge." "It is true, Madam," replied he, "I was there without your orders, and I passed there the most sweet and cruel moments of my life."

Madam de Cleves understood very well what he said, but made him no answer; her care was to prevent Madam de Mercoeur from going into the bower, because the Duke de Nemours's picture was there, and she had no mind she should see it; she managed the matter so well, that the time passed away insensibly, and Madam de Mercoeur began to talk of going home: but when Madam de Cleves found that the Duke and his sister did not go together, she plainly saw to what she was going to be exposed; she found herself under the same embarrassment she was in at Paris, and took also the same resolution; her fear, lest this visit should be a further confirmation of her husband's suspicions, did not a little contribute to determine her; and to the end Monsieur de Nemours might not remain alone with her, she told Madam de Mercoeur she would wait upon her to the borders of the forest, and ordered her chariot to be got ready. The Duke was struck with such a violent grief to find that Madam de Cleves still continued to exercise the same rigours towards him, that he turned pale that moment. Madam de Mercoeur asked him if he was ill, but he looked upon Madam de Cleves without being perceived by anybody else, and made her sensible by his looks that he had no other illness besides despair: however, there was no remedy but he must let them go together without daring to follow them; after what he had told his sister, that he was to go directly to Court, he could not return with her, but went to Paris, and set out from thence the next day.

Monsieur de Cleves's gentleman had observed him all the while; he returned also to Paris, and when he found Monsieur de Nemours was set out for Chambort, he took post to get thither before him, and to give an account of his journey; his master expected his return with impatience, as if the happiness or unhappiness of his life depended upon it.

As soon as he saw him, he judged from his countenance and his silence, that the news he brought was very disagreeable; he was struck with sorrow, and continued some time with his head hung down, without being able to speak; at last he made signs with his hand to him to withdraw; "Go," says he, "I see what you have to say to me, but I have not the power to hear it." "I can acquaint you with nothing," said the gentleman, "upon which one can form any certain judgment; it is true, the Duke de Nemours went two nights successively into the garden in the forest, and the day after he was at Colomiers with the Duchess of Mercoeur." "'Tis enough," replied Monsieur de Cleves, still making signs to him to withdraw, "'tis enough; I want no further information." The gentleman was forced to leave his master, abandoned to his despair; nor ever was despair more violent. Few men of so high a spirit, and so passionately in love, as the Prince of Cleves, have experienced at the same time the grief arising from the falsehood of a mistress, and the shame of being deceived by a wife.

Monsieur de Cleves could set no bounds to his affliction; he felt ill of a fever that very night, and his distemper was accompanied with such ill symptoms that it was thought very dangerous. Madam de Cleves was informed of it, and came in all haste to him; when she arrived, he was still worse; besides, she observed something in him so cold and chilling with respect to her, that she was equally surprised and grieved at it; he even seemed to receive with pain the services she did him in his sickness, but at last she imagined it was perhaps only the effect of his distemper.

When she was come to Blois where the Court then was, the Duke de Nemours was overjoyed to think she was at the same place where he was; he endeavoured to see her, and went every day to the Prince of Cleves's under pretence of enquiring how he did, but it was to no purpose; she did not stir out of her husband's room, and was grieved at heart for the condition he was in. It vexed Monsieur de Nemours to see her under such affliction, an affliction which he plainly saw revived the friendship she had for Monsieur de Cleves, and diverted the passion that lay kindling in her heart. The thought of this shocked him severely for some time; but the extremity, to which Monsieur de Cleves's sickness was grown, opened to him a scene of new hopes; he saw it was probable that Madam de Cleves would be at liberty to follow her own inclinations, and that he might expect for the future a series of happiness and lasting pleasures; he could not support the ecstasy of that thought, a thought so full of transport! he banished it out of his mind for fear of becoming doubly wretched, if he happened to be disappointed in his hopes.

In the meantime Monsieur de Cleves was almost given over by his physicians. One of the last days of his illness, after having had a very bad night, he said in the morning, he had a desire to sleep; but Madam de Cleves, who remained alone in his chamber, found that instead of taking repose he was extremely restless; she came to him, and fell on her knees by his bedside, her face all covered with tears; and though Monsieur de Cleves had taken a resolution not to show her the violent displeasure he had conceived against her, yet the care she took of him, and the sorrow she expressed, which sometimes he thought sincere, and at other times the effect of her dissimulation and perfidiousness, distracted him so violently with opposite sentiments full of woe, that he could not forbear giving them vent.

"You shed plenty of tears, Madam," said he, "for a death which you are the cause of, and which cannot give you the trouble you pretend to be in; I am no longer in a condition to reproach you," added he with a voice weakened by sickness and grief; "I die through the dreadful grief and discontent you have given me; ought so extraordinary an action, as that of your speaking to me at Colomiers, to have had so little consequences? Why did you inform me of your passion for the Duke de Nemours, if your virtue was no longer able to oppose it? I loved you to that extremity, I would have been glad to have been deceived, I confess it to my shame; I have regretted that pleasing false security out of which you drew me; why did not you leave me in that blind tranquillity which so many husbands enjoy? I should perhaps have been ignorant all my life, that you was in love with Monsieur de Nemours; I shall die," added he, "but know that you make death pleasing to me, and that, after you have taken from me the esteem and affection I had for you, life would be odious to me. What should I live for? to spend my days with a person whom I have loved so much, and by whom I have been so cruelly deceived; or to live apart from her and break out openly into violences so opposite to my temper, and the love I had for you? That love, Madam, was far greater than it appeared to you; I concealed the greatest part of it from you, for fear of being importunate, or of losing somewhat in your esteem by a behaviour not becoming a husband: in a word, I deserved your affection more than once, and I die without regret, since I have not been able to obtain it, and since I can no longer desire it. Adieu, Madam; you will one day regret a man who loved you with a sincere and virtuous passion; you will feel the anxiety which reasonable persons meet with in intrigue and gallantry, and you will know the difference between such a love as I had for you, and the love of people who only profess admiration for you to gratify their vanity in seducing you; but my death will leave you at liberty, and you may make the Duke de Nemours happy without guilt: what signifies anything that can happen when I am no more, and why should I have the weakness to trouble myself about it?"

Madam de Cleves was so far from imagining that her husband suspected her virtue, that she heard all this discourse without comprehending the meaning of it, and without having any other notion about it, except that he reproached her for her inclination for the Duke de Nemours; at last, starting all of a sudden out of her blindness, "I guilty!" cried she, "I am a stranger to the very thought of guilt; the severest virtue could not have inspired any other conduct than that which I have followed, and I never acted anything but what I could have wished you to have been witness to." "Could you have wished," replied Monsieur de Cleves, looking on her with disdain, "I had been a witness of those nights you passed with Monsieur de Nemours? Ah! Madam; is it you I speak of, when I speak of a lady that has passed nights with a man, not her husband?" "No, sir," replied she, "it is not me you speak of; I never spent a night nor a moment with the Duke de Nemours; he never saw me in private, I never suffered him to do it, nor would give him a hearing. I'll take all the oaths . . ." "Speak no more of it," said he interrupting her, "false oaths or a confession would perhaps give me equal pain."

Madam de Cleves could not answer him; her tears and her grief took away her speech; at last, struggling for utterance, "Look on me at least, hear me," said she; "if my interest only were concerned I would suffer these reproaches, but your life is at stake; hear me for your own sake; I am so innocent, truth pleads so strongly for me, it is impossible but I must convince you." "Would to God you could!" cried he; "but what can you say? the Duke de Nemours, has not he been at Colomiers with his sister? And did not he pass the two foregoing nights with you in the garden in the forest?" "If that be my crime," replied she, "it is easy to justify myself; I do not desire you to believe me, believe your servants and domestics; ask them if I went into the garden the evening before Monsieur de Nemours came to Colomiers, and if I did not go out, of it the night before two hours sooner than I used to do." After this she told him how she imagined she had seen somebody in the garden, and acknowledged that she believed it to be the Duke de Nemours; she spoke to him with so much confidence, and truth so naturally persuades, even where it is not probable, that Monsieur de Cleves was almost convinced of her innocence. "I don't know," said he, "whether I ought to believe you; I am so near death, that I would not know anything that might make me die with reluctance; you have cleared your innocence too late; however it will be a comfort to me to go away with the thought that you are worthy of the esteem I have had for you; I beg you I may be assured of this further comfort, that my memory will be dear to you, and that if it had been in your power you would have had for me the same passion which you had for another." He would have gone on, but was so weak that his speech failed him. Madam de Cleves sent for the physicians, who found him almost lifeless; yet he languished some days, and died at last with admirable constancy.

Madam de Cleves was afflicted to so violent a degree, that she lost in a manner the use of her reason; the Queen was so kind as to come to see her, and carried her to a convent without her being sensible whither she was conducted; her sisters-in-law brought her back to Paris, before she was in a condition to feel distinctly even her griefs: when she was restored to her faculty of thinking, and reflected what a husband she had lost, and considered that she had caused his death by the passion which she had for another, the horror she had for herself and the Duke de Nemours was not to be expressed.

The Duke in the beginning of her mourning durst pay her no other respects but such as decency required; he knew Madam de Cleves enough to be sensible that great importunities and eagerness would be disagreeable to her; but what he learned afterwards plainly convinced him that he ought to observe the same conduct a great while longer.

A servant of the Duke's informed him that Monsieur de Cleves's gentleman, who was his intimate friend, had told him, in the excess of his grief for the loss of his master, that Monsieur de Nemours's journey to Colomiers was the occasion of his death. The Duke was extremely surprised to hear this; but after having reflected upon it, he guessed the truth in part, and rightly judged what Madam de Cleves's sentiments would be at first, and what a distance it would throw him from her, if she thought her husband's illness was occasioned by his jealousy; he was of opinion that he ought not so much as to put her in mind of his name very soon, and he abided by that conduct, however severe it appeared to him.

He took a journey to Paris, nor could he forbear calling at her house to enquire how she did. He was told, that she saw nobody, and that she had even given strict orders that they should not trouble her with an account of any that might come to see her; those very strict orders, perhaps, were given with a view to the Duke, and to prevent her hearing him spoken of; but he was too much in love to be able to live so absolutely deprived of the sight of Madam de Cleves; he resolved to find the means, let the difficulty be what it would, to get out of a condition which was so insupportable to him.

The grief of that Princess exceeded the bounds of reason; a husband dying, and dying on her account, and with so much tenderness for her, never went out of her mind: she continually revolved in her thoughts what she owed him, and she condemned herself for not having had a passion for him, as if that had been a thing which depended on herself; she found no consolation but in the thought that she lamented him as he deserved to be lamented, and that she would do nothing during the remainder of her life, but what he would have been glad she should have done, had he lived.

She had often been thinking how he came to know, that the Duke de Nemours had been at Colomiers; she could not suspect that the Duke himself had told it; though it was indifferent to her whether he had or no, she thought herself so perfectly cured of the passion she had had for him; and yet she was grieved at the heart to think that he was the cause of her husband's death; and she remembered with pain the fear Monsieur de Cleves expressed, when dying, lest she should marry the Duke; but all these griefs were swallowed up in that for the loss of her husband, and she thought she had no other but that one.

After several months the violence of her grief abated, and she fell into a languishing kind of melancholy. Madam de Martigues made a journey to Paris, and constantly visited her during the time she stayed there: she entertained her with an account of the Court, and what passed there; and though Madam de Cleves appeared unconcerned, yet still she continued talking on that subject in hopes to divert her.

She talked to her of the Viscount, of Monsieur de Guise, and of all others that were distinguished either in person or merit. "As for the Duke de Nemours," says she, "I don't know if State affairs have not taken possession of his heart in the room of gallantry; he is abundantly less gay than he used to be, and seems wholly to decline the company of women; he often makes journeys to Paris, and I believe he is there now." The Duke de Nemours's name surprised Madam de Cleves, and made her blush; she changed the discourse, nor did Madam de Martigues take notice of her concern.

The next day Madam de Cleves, who employed herself in things suitable to the condition she was in, went to a man's house in her neighbourhood, that was famous for working silk after a particular manner, and she designed to bespeak some pieces for herself; having seen several kinds of his work, she spied a chamber door, where she thought there were more, and desired it might be opened: the master answered, he had not the key, and that the room was taken by a man, who came there sometimes in the daytime to draw the plans and prospects of the fine houses and gardens that were to be seen from his windows; "he is one of the handsomest men I ever saw," added he, "and does not look much like one that works for his living; whenever he comes here, I observe he always looks towards the gardens and houses, but I never see him work."

Madam de Cleves listened to this story very attentively, and what Madam de Martigues had told her of Monsieur de Nemours's coming now and then to Paris, she applied in her fancy to that handsome man, who came to a place so near her house; and this gave her an idea of Monsieur de Nemours endeavouring to see her; which raised a disorder in her, of which she did not know the cause: she went towards the windows to see where they looked into, and she found they overlooked all her gardens, and directly faced her apartment: and when she was in her own room, she could easily see that very window where she was told the man came to take his prospects. The thought that it was the Duke de Nemours, entirely changed the situation of her mind; she no longer found herself in that pensive tranquillity which she had begun to enjoy, her spirits were ruffled again as with a tempest: at last, not being able to stay at home, she went abroad to take the air in a garden without the suburbs, where she hoped to be alone; she walked about a great while, and found no likelihood of anyone's being there.

Having crossed a little wilderness she perceived at the end of the walk, in the most remote part of the garden, a kind of a bower, open on all sides, and went towards it; when she was near, she saw a man lying on the benches, who seemed sunk into a deep contemplation, and she discovered it was the Duke de Nemours. Upon this she stopped short: but her attendants made some noise, which roused the Duke out of his musing: he took no notice who the persons were that disturbed him, but got up in order to avoid the company that was coming towards him, and making a low bow, which hindered him from seeing those he saluted, he turned into another walk.

If he had known whom he avoided, with what eagerness would he have returned? But he walked down the alley, and Madam de Cleves saw him go out at a back door, where his coach waited for him. What an effect did this transient view produce in the heart of Madam de Cleves? What a flame rekindled out of the embers of her love, and with what violence did it burn? She went and sat down in the same place from which Monsieur de Nemours was newly risen, and seemed perfectly overwhelmed; his image immediately possessed her fancy, and she considered him as the most amiable person in the world, as one who had long loved her with a passion full of veneration and sincerity, slighting all for her, paying respect even to her grief, to his own torture, labouring to see her without a thought of being seen by her, quitting the Court (though the Court's delight) to come and look on the walls where she was shut up, and to pass his melancholy hours in places where he could not hope to meet her; in a word, a man whose attachment to her alone merited returns of love, and for whom she had so strong an inclination, that she should have loved him, though she had not been beloved by him; and besides, one whose quality was suitable to hers: all the obstacles that could rise from duty and virtue were now removed, and all the trace that remained on her mind of their former condition was the passion the Duke de Nemours had for her, and that which she had for him.

All these ideas were new to her; her affliction for the death of her husband had left her no room for thoughts of this kind, but the sight of Monsieur de Nemours revived them, and they crowded again into her mind; but when she had taken her fill of them, and remembered that this very man, whom she considered as a proper match for her, was the same she had loved in her husband's lifetime, and was the cause of his death, and that on his death-bed he had expressed a fear of her marrying him, her severe virtue was so shocked at the imagination, that she thought it would be as criminal in her to marry Monsieur de Nemours now, as it was to love him before: in short, she abandoned herself to these reflections so pernicious to her happiness, and fortified herself in them by the inconveniency which she foresaw would attend such a marriage. After two hours' stay in this place she returned home, convinced that it was indispensably her duty to avoid the sight of the man she loved.

But this conviction, which was the effect of reason and virtue, did not carry her heart along with it; her heart was so violently fixed on the Duke de Nemours, that she became even an object of compassion, and was wholly deprived of rest. Never did she pass a night in so uneasy a manner; in the morning, the first thing she did was to see if there was anybody at the window which looked towards her apartment; she saw there Monsieur de Nemours, and was so surprised upon it, and withdrew so hastily, as made him judge she knew him; he had often wished to be seen by her, ever since he had found out that method of seeing her, and when he had no hopes of obtaining that satisfaction, his way was to go to muse in the garden where she found him.

Tired at last with so unfortunate and uncertain a condition, he resolved to attempt something to determine his fate: "What should I wait for?" said he. "I have long known she loves me; she is free; she has no duty now to plead against me; why should I submit myself to the hardship of seeing her, without being seen by her or speaking to her? Is it possible for love so absolutely to have deprived me of reason and courage, and to have rendered me so different from what I have been in all my other amours? It was fit I should pay a regard to Madam de Cleves's grief; but I do it too long, and I give her leisure to extinguish the inclination she had for me."

After these reflections, he considered what measures he ought to take to see her; he found he had no longer any reason to conceal his passion from the Viscount de Chartres; he resolved to speak to him of it, and to communicate to him his design with regard to his niece.

The Viscount was then at Paris, the town being extremely full, and everybody busy in preparing equipages and dresses to attend the King of Navarre, who was to conduct the Queen of Spain: Monsieur de Nemours, went to the Viscount, and made an ingenuous confession to him of all he had concealed hitherto, except Madam de Cleves's sentiments, which he would not seem to know.

The Viscount received what he told him with a great deal of pleasure, and assured him, that though he was not acquainted with his sentiments on that subject, he had often thought, since Madam de Cleves had been a widow, that she was the only lady that deserved him. Monsieur de Nemours entreated him to give him an opportunity of speaking to her, and learning what disposition she was in.

The Viscount proposed to carry him to her house, but the Duke was of opinion she would be shocked at it, because as yet she saw nobody; so that they agreed, it would be better for the Viscount to ask her to come to him, under some pretence, and for the Duke to come to them by a private staircase, that he might not be observed. Accordingly this was executed; Madam de Cleves came, the Viscount went to receive her, and led her into a great closet at the end of his apartment; some time after Monsieur de Nemours came in, as by chance: Madam de Cleves was in great surprise to see him; she blushed and endeavoured to hide it; the Viscount at first spoke of indifferent matters, and then went out, as if he had some orders to give, telling Madam de Cleves he must desire her to entertain the Duke in his stead, and that he would return immediately.

It is impossible to express the sentiments of Monsieur de Nemours, and Madam de Cleves, when they saw themselves alone, and at liberty to speak to one another, as they had never been before: they continued silent a while; at length, said Monsieur de Nemours, "Can you, Madam, pardon the Viscount for giving me an opportunity of seeing you, and speaking to you, an opportunity which you have always so cruelly denied me?" "I ought not to pardon him," replied she, "for having forgot the condition I am in, and to what he exposes my reputation." Having spoke these words, she would have gone away; but Monsieur de Nemours stopping her, "Fear not, Madam," said he; "you have nothing to apprehend; nobody knows I am here; hear me, Madam, hear me, if not out of goodness, yet at least for your own sake, and to free yourself from the extravagancies which a passion I am no longer master of will infallibly hurry me into." Madam de Cleves now first yielded to the inclination she had for the Duke de Nemours, and beholding him with eyes full of softness and charms, "But what can you hope for," says she, "from the complaisance you desire of me? You will perhaps repent that you have obtained it, and I shall certainly repent that I have granted it. You deserve a happier fortune than you have hitherto had, or than you can have for the future, unless you seek it elsewhere." "I, Madam," said he, "seek happiness anywhere else? Or is there any happiness for me, but in your love? Though I never spoke of it before, I cannot believe, Madam, that you are not acquainted with my passion, or that you do not know it to be the greatest and most sincere that ever was; what trials has it suffered in things you are a stranger to? What trials have you put it to by your rigour?"

"Since you are desirous I should open myself to you," answered Madam de Cleves, "I'll comply with your desire, and I'll do it with a sincerity that is rarely to be met with in persons of my sex: I shall not tell you that I have not observed your passion for me; perhaps you would not believe me if I should tell you so; I confess therefore to you, not only that I have observed it, but that I have observed it in such lights as you yourself could wish it might appear to me in." "And if you have seen my passion, Madam," said he, "is it possible for you not to have been moved by it? And may I venture to ask, if it has made no impression on your heart?" "You should have judged of that from my conduct," replied she; "but I should be glad to know what you thought of it." "I ought to be in a happier condition," replied he, "to venture to inform you; my fortune would contradict what I should say; all I can tell you, Madam, is that I heartily wished you had not acknowledged to Monsieur de Cleves what you concealed from me, and that you had concealed from him what you made appear to me." "How came you to discover," replied she blushing, "that I acknowledged anything to Monsieur de Cleves?" "I learned it from yourself, Madam," replied he; "but that you may the better pardon the boldness I showed in listening to what you said, remember if I have made an ill use of what I heard, if my hopes rose upon it, or if I was the more encouraged to speak to you."

Here he began to relate how he had overheard her conversation with Monsieur de Cleves; but she interrupted him before he had finished; "Say no more of it," said she, "I see how you came to be so well informed; I suspected you knew the business but too well at the Queen-Dauphin's, who learned this adventure from those you had entrusted with it."

Upon this Monsieur de Nemours informed her in what manner the thing came to pass; "No excuses," says she; "I have long forgiven you, without being informed how it was brought about; but since you have learned from my ownself what I designed to conceal from you all my life, I will acknowledge to you that you have inspired me with sentiments I was unacquainted with before I saw you, and of which I had so slender an idea, that they gave me at first a surprise which still added to the pain that constantly attends them: I am the less ashamed to make you this confession, because I do it at a time when I may do it without a crime, and because you have seen that my conduct has not been governed by my affections."

"Can you believe, Madam," said Monsieur de Nemours, falling on his knees, "but I shall expire at your feet with joy and transport?" "I have told you nothing," said she smiling, "but what you knew too well before." "Ah! Madam," said he, "what a difference is there between learning it by chance, and knowing it from yourself, and seeing withal that you are pleased I know it." "It is true," answered she, "I would have you know it, and I find a pleasure in telling it you; I don't even know if I do not tell it you more for my own sake, than for yours; for, after all, this confession will have no consequences, and I shall follow the austere rules which my duty imposes upon me." "How! Madam; you are not of this opinion," replied Monsieur de Nemours; "you are no longer under any obligation of duty; you are at liberty; and if I durst, I should even tell you, that it is in your power to act so, that your duty shall one day oblige you to preserve the sentiments you have for me." "My duty," replied she, "forbids me to think of any man, but of you the last in the world, and for reasons which are unknown to you." "Those reasons perhaps are not unknown to me," answered he, "but they are far from being good ones. I believe that Monsieur de Cleves thought me happier than I was, and imagined that you approved of those extravagancies which my passion led me into without your approbation." "Let us talk no more of that adventure," said she; "I cannot bear the thought of it, it giving me shame, and the consequences of it have been such that it is too melancholy a subject to be spoken of; it is but too true that you were the cause of Monsieur de Cleves's death; the suspicions which your inconsiderate conduct gave him, cost him his life as much as if you had taken it away with your own hands: judge what I ought to have done, had you two fought a duel, and he been killed; I know very well, it is not the same thing in the eye of the world, but with me there's no difference, since I know that his death was owing to you, and that it was on my account." "Ah! Madam," said Monsieur de Nemours, "what phantom of duty do you oppose to my happiness? What! Madam, shall a vain and groundless fancy hinder you from making a man happy, for whom you have an inclination? What, have I had some ground to hope I might pass my life with you? has my fate led me to love the most deserving lady in the world? have I observed in her all that can make a mistress adorable? Has she had no disliking to me? Have I found in her conduct everything which perhaps I could wish for in a wife? For in short, Madam, you are perhaps the only person in whom those two characters have ever concurred to the degree they are in you; those who marry mistresses, by whom they are loved, tremble when they marry them, and cannot but fear lest they should observe the same conduct towards others which they observed towards them; but in you, Madam, I can fear nothing, I see nothing in you but matter of admiration: have I had a prospect of so much felicity for no other end but to see it obstructed by you? Ah! Madam, you forget, that you have distinguished me above other men; or rather, you have not distinguished me; you have deceived yourself, and I have flattered myself."

"You have not flattered yourself," replied she; "the reasons of my duty would not perhaps appear so strong to me without that distinction of which you doubt, and it is that which makes me apprehend unfortunate consequences from your alliance." "I have nothing to answer, Madam," replied he, "when you tell me you apprehend unfortunate consequences; but I own, that after all you have been pleased to say to me, I did not expect from you so cruel a reason." "The reason you speak of," replied Madam de Cleves, "is so little disobliging as to you, that I don't know how to tell it you." "Alas! Madam," said he, "how can you fear I should flatter myself too much after what you have been saying to me?" "I shall continue to speak to you," says she, "with the same sincerity with which I begun, and I'll lay aside that delicacy and reserve that modesty obliges one to in a first conversation, but I conjure you to hear me without interruption.

"I think I owe the affection you have for me, the poor recompsense not to hide from you any of my thoughts, and to let you see them such as they really are; this in all probability will be the only time I shall allow myself the freedom to discover them to you; and I cannot confess without a blush, that the certainty of not being loved by you, as I am, appears to me so dreadful a misfortune, that if I had not invincible reasons grounded on my duty, I could not resolve to subject myself to it; I know that you are free, that I am so too, and that circumstances are such, that the public perhaps would have no reason to blame either you or me, should we unite ourselves forever; but do men continue to love, when under engagements for life? Ought I to expect a miracle in my favour? And shall I place myself in a condition of seeing certainly that passion come to an end, in which I should place all my felicity? Monsieur de Cleves was perhaps the only man in the world capable of continuing to love after marriage; it was my ill fate that I was not able to enjoy that happiness, and perhaps his passion had not lasted but that he found none, in me; but I should not have the same way of preserving yours; I even think your constancy is owing to the obstacles you have met with; you have met with enough to animate you to conquer them; and my unguarded actions, or what you learned by chance, gave you hopes enough not to be discouraged." "Ah! Madam," replied Monsieur de Nemours, "I cannot keep the silence you enjoined me; you do me too much injustice, and make it appear too clearly that you are far from being prepossessed in my favour." "I confess," answered she, "that my passions may lead me, but they cannot blind me; nothing can hinder me from knowing that you are born with a disposition for gallantry, and have all the qualities proper to give success; you have already had a great many amours, and you will have more; I should no longer be she you placed your happiness in; I should see you as warm for another as you had been for me; this would grievously vex me, and I am not sure I should not have the torment of jealousy; I have said too much to conceal from you that you have already made me know what jealousy is, and that I suffered such cruel inquietudes the evening the Queen gave me Madam de Themines's letter, which it was said was addressed to you, that to this moment I retain an idea of it, which makes me believe it is the worst of all ills.

"There is scarce a woman but out of vanity or inclination desires to engage you; there are very few whom you do not please, and my own experience would make me believe, that there are none whom it is not in your power to please; I should think you always in love and beloved, nor should I be often mistaken; and yet in this case I should have no remedy but patience, nay I question if I should dare to complain: a lover may be reproached; but can a husband be so, when one has nothing to urge, but that he loves one no longer? But admit I could accustom myself to bear a misfortune of this nature, yet how could I bear that of imagining I constantly saw Monsieur de Cleves, accusing you of his death, reproaching me with having loved you, with having married you, and showing me the difference betwixt his affection and yours? It is impossible to over-rule such strong reasons as these; I must continue in the condition I am in, and in the resolution I have taken never to alter it." "Do you believe you have the power to do it, Madam?" cried the Duke de Nemours. "Do you think your resolution can hold out against a man who adores, and who has the happiness to please you? It is more difficult than you imagine, Madam, to resist a person who pleases and loves one at the same time; you have done it by an austerity of virtue, which is almost without example; but that virtue no longer opposes your inclinations, and I hope you will follow them in spite of yourself." "I know nothing can be more difficult than what I undertake," replied Madam de Cleves; "I distrust my strength in the midst of my reasons; what I think I owe to the memory of Monsieur de Cleves would be a weak consideration, if not supported by the interest of my ease and repose; and the reasons of my repose have need to be supported by those of my duty; but though I distrust myself, I believe I shall never overcome my scruples, nor do I so much as hope to overcome the inclination I have for you; that inclination will make me unhappy, and I will deny myself the sight of you, whatever violence it is to me: I conjure you, by all the power I have over you, to seek no occasion of seeing me; I am in a condition which makes that criminal which might be lawful at another time; decency forbids all commerce between us." Monsieur de Nemours threw himself at her feet, and gave a loose to all the violent motions with which he was agitated; he expressed both by his words and tears the liveliest and most tender passion that ever heart was touched with; nor was the heart of Madam de Cleves insensible; she looked upon him with eyes swelled with tears: "Why was it," cries she, "that I can charge you with Monsieur de Cleves's death? Why did not my first acquaintance with you begin since I have been at liberty, or why did not I know you before I was engaged? Why does fate separate us by such invincible obstacles?" "There are no obstacles, Madam," replied Monsieur de Nemours; "it is you alone oppose my happiness; you impose on yourself a law which virtue and reason do not require you to obey." "'Tis true," says she, "I sacrifice a great deal to a duty which does not subsist but in my imagination; have patience, and expect what time may produce; Monsieur de Cleves is but just expired, and that mournful object is too near to leave me clear and distinct views; in the meantime enjoy the satisfaction to know you have gained the heart of a person who would never have loved anyone, had she not seen you: believe the inclination I have for you will last forever, and that it will be uniform and the same, whatever becomes of me: Adieu," said she; "this is a conversation I ought to blush for; however, give an account of it to the Viscount; I agree to it, and desire you to do it."

With these words she went away, nor could Monsieur de Nemours detain her. In the next room she met with the Viscount, who seeing her under so much concern would not speak to her, but led her to her coach without saying a word; he returned to Monsieur de Nemours, who was so full of joy, grief, admiration, and of all those affections that attend a passion full of hope and fear, that he had not the use of his reason. It was a long time ere the Viscount could get from him an account of the conversation; at last the Duke related it to him, and Monsieur de Chartres, without being in love, no less admired the virtue, wit and merit of Madam de Cleves, than did Monsieur de Nemours himself; they began to examine what issue could reasonably be hoped for in this affair; and however fearful the Duke de Nemours was from his love, he agreed with the Viscount, that it was impossible Madam de Cleves should continue in the resolution she was in; they were of opinion nevertheless that it was necessary to follow her orders, for fear, upon the public's perceiving the inclination he had for her, she should make declarations and enter into engagements with respect to the world, that she would afterwards abide by, lest it should be thought she loved him in her husband's lifetime.

Monsieur de Nemours determined to follow the King; it was a journey he could not well excuse himself from, and so he resolved to go without endeavouring to see Madam de Cleves again from the window out of which he had sometimes seen her; he begged the Viscount to speak to her; and what did he not desire him to say in his behalf? What an infinite number of reasons did he furnish him with, to persuade her to conquer her scruples? In short, great part of the night was spent before he thought of going away.

As for Madam de Cleves, she was in no condition to rest; it was a thing so new to her to have broke loose from the restraints she had laid on herself, to have endured the first declarations of love that ever were made to her, and to have confessed that she herself was in love with him that made them, all this was so new to her, that she seemed quite another person; she was surprised at what she had done; she repented of it; she was glad of it; all her thoughts were full of anxiety and passion; she examined again the reasons of her duty, which obstructed her happiness; she was grieved to find them so strong, and was sorry that she had made them out so clear to Monsieur de Nemours: though she had entertained thoughts of marrying him, as soon as she beheld him in the garden of the suburbs, yet her late conversation with him made a much greater impression on her mind; at some moments she could not comprehend how she could be unhappy by marrying him, and she was ready to say in her heart, that her scruples as to what was past, and her fears for the future, were equally groundless: at other times, reason and her duty prevailed in her thoughts, and violently hurried her into a resolution not to marry again, and never to see Monsieur de Nemours; but this was a resolution hard to be established in a heart so softened as hers, and so lately abandoned to the charms of love. At last, to give herself a little ease, she concluded that it was not yet necessary to do herself the violence of coming to any resolution, and decency allowed her a considerable time to determine what to do: however she resolved to continue firm in having no commerce with Monsieur de Nemours. The Viscount came to see her, and pleaded his friend's cause with all the wit and application imaginable, but could not make her alter her conduct, or recall the severe orders she had given to Monsieur de Nemours; she told him her design was not to change her condition; that she knew how difficult it was to stand to that design, but that she hoped she should be able to do it; she made him so sensible how far she was affected with the opinion that Monsieur de Nemours was the cause of her husband's death, and how much she was convinced that it would be contrary to her duty to marry him, that the Viscount was afraid it would be very difficult to take away those impressions; he did not, however, tell the Duke what he thought, when he gave him an account of his conversation with her, but left him as much hope as a man who is loved may reasonably have.

They set out the next day, and went after the King; the Viscount wrote to Madam de Cleves at Monsieur de Nemours's request, and in a second letter, which soon followed the first, the Duke wrote a line or two in his own hand; but Madam de Cleves determined not to depart from the rules she had prescribed herself, and fearing the accidents that might happen from letters, informed the Viscount that she would receive his letters no more, if he continued to speak of Monsieur de Nemours, and did it in so peremptory a manner, that the Duke desired him not to mention him.

During the absence of the Court, which was gone to conduct the Queen of Spain as far as Poitou, Madam de Cleves continued at home; and the more distant she was from Monsieur de Nemours, and from everything that could put her in mind of him, the more she recalled the memory of the Prince of Cleves, which she made it her glory to preserve; the reasons she had not to marry the Duke de Nemours appeared strong with respect to her duty, but invincible with respect to her quiet; the opinion she had, that marriage would put an end to his love, and the torments of jealousy, which she thought the infallible consequences of marriage, gave her the prospect of a certain unhappiness if she consented to his desires; on the other hand, she thought it impossible, if he were present, to refuse the most amiable man in the world, the man who loved her, and whom she loved, and to oppose him in a thing that was neither inconsistent with virtue nor decency: she thought that nothing but absence and distance could give her the power to do it; and she found she stood in need of them, not only to support her resolution not to marry, but even to keep her from seeing Monsieur de Nemours; she resolved therefore to take a long journey, in order to pass away the time which decency obliged her to spend in retirement; the fine estate she had near the Pyrenees seemed the most proper place she could make choice of; she set out a few days before the Court returned, and wrote at parting to the Viscount to conjure him not to think of once enquiring after her, or of writing to her.

Monsieur de Nemours was as much troubled at this journey as another would have been for the death of his mistress; the thought of being deprived so long a time of the sight of Madam de Cleves grieved him to the soul, especially as it happened at a time when he had lately enjoyed the pleasure of seeing her, and of seeing her moved by his passion; however he could do nothing but afflict himself, and his affliction increased every day. Madam de Cleves, whose spirits had been so much agitated, was no sooner arrived at her country seat, but she fell desperately ill; the news of it was brought to Court; Monsieur de Nemours was inconsolable; his grief proceeded even to despair and extravagance; the Viscount had much a-do to hinder him from discovering his passion in public, and as much a-do to keep him from going in person to know how she did; the relation and friendship between her and the Viscount served as an excuse for sending frequent messengers; at last they heard she was out of the extremity of danger she had been in, but continued in a languishing malady that left but little hopes of life.

The nature of her disease gave her a prospect of death both near, and at a distance, and showed her the things of this life in a very different view from that in which they are seen by people in health; the necessity of dying, to which she saw herself so near, taught her to wean herself from the world, and the lingeringness of her distemper brought her to a habit in it; yet when she was a little recovered, she found that Monsieur de Nemours was not effaced from her heart; but to defend herself against him, she called to her aid all the reasons which she thought she had never to marry him; after a long conflict in herself, she subdued the relics of that passion which had been weakened by the sentiments her illness had given her; the thoughts of death had reproached her with the memory of Monsieur de Cleves, and this remembrance was so agreeable to her duty, that it made deep impressions in her heart; the passions and engagements of the world appeared to her in the light, in which they appear to persons who have more great and more distant views. The weakness of her body, which was brought very low, aided her in preserving these sentiments; but as she knew what power opportunities have over the wisest resolutions, she would not hazard the breach of those she had taken, by returning into any place where she might see him she loved; she retired, under pretence of change of air, into a convent, but without declaring a settled resolution of quitting the Court.

Upon the first news of it, Monsieur de Nemours felt the weight of this retreat, and saw the importance of it; he presently thought he had nothing more to hope, but omitted not anything that might oblige her to return; he prevailed with the Queen to write; he made the Viscount not only write, but go to her, but all to no purpose; the Viscount saw her, but she did not tell him she had fixed her resolution; and yet he judged, she would never return to Court; at last Monsieur de Nemours himself went to her, under pretence of using the waters; she was extremely grieved and surprised to hear he was come, and sent him word by a person of merit about her, that she desired him not to take it ill if she did not expose herself to the danger of seeing him, and of destroying by his presence those sentiments she was obliged to preserve; that she desired he should know, that having found it both against her duty and peace of mind to yield to the inclination she had to be his, all things else were become so indifferent to her, that she had renounced them for ever; that she thought only of another life, and had no sentiment remaining as to this, but the desire of seeing him in the same dispositions she was in.

Monsieur de Nemours was like to have expired in the presence of the lady who told him this; he begged her a thousand times to return to Madam de Cleves, and to get leave for him to see her; but she told him the Princess had not only forbidden her to come back with any message from him, but even to report the conversation that should pass between them. At length Monsieur de Nemours was obliged to go back, oppressed with the heaviest grief a man is capable of, who has lost all hopes of ever seeing again a person, whom he loved not only with the most violent, but most natural and sincere passion that ever was; yet still he was not utterly discouraged, but used all imaginable methods to make her alter her resolution; at last, after several years, time and absence abated his grief, and extinguished his passion. Madam de Cleves lived in a manner that left no probability of her ever returning to Court; she spent one part of the year in that religious house, and the other at her own, but still continued the austerity of retirement, and constantly employed herself in exercises more holy than the severest convents can pretend to; and her life, though it was short, left examples of inimitable virtues.

Milton Keynes UK
Ingram Content Group UK Ltd.
UKHW030625061024
449204UK00004B/304

9 789362 091048